Bismi Llahi r-Rahmani r-Rahim

In the name of Allah the Most Compassionate, the Most Merciful.

We have told you the stories of the prophets to make your heart firm and in these accounts, truth has come to you, as well as lessons and reminders for the believers. (11:120)

Indeed, in the stories of these men there is a lesson for those who are endowed with insight. (12:111)

The disbelievers say, 'These are nothing but ancient fables,' (6:25)

Other Titles By This Author:

My Little Lore of Light
The Light of Muhammad
Links of Light: The Golden Chain
The Story of Moses
Who Are You? A Book of Very Serious Questions
The Animals of Paradise
The Animals of Paradise: Coloring Book
My Little Lore of Light: Coloring Book
Every Day A Thousand Times
As-Salamu 'Alaykum Ya Rasul Allah (sas)
Ibrahim Khalil Allah (as)
Animal Salams
A Book of Angels
The Family of 'Imran: Mary, Jesus, Zachariah and John

Copyright © 2022 by Karima Sperling
All rights reserved. This book or any portion thereof may not be reproduced or used in any manner whatsoever without the express written permission of the publisher except for the use of brief quotations in a book review.
Printed in the United States of America 979-8-218-02482-6
Little Bird Books littlebirdbooksink@gmail.com

Following Moses (as):

The Story of Joshua (as)

By Karima Sperling

Dedication

To Shaykh Muhammad Nazim al-Haqqani and Shaykh Mehmet Adil al-Haqqani, father and son, shaykh and faithful inheritor, trustworthy guides on the Middle Way.

Thank You

To Mawlana Shaykh Nazim al-Haqqani (q) who gifted me with this task.
To Shaykh Mehmet Efendi for suggesting Yusha' (as) and for continuous spiritual support.
To Shaykh Bahauddin for inspiration.
To Hajja Rukiye Sultan for stories for the heart and food for the soul. And for deciphering many a calligraphical mystery.
To Hajj Mehmet Nazim for being a source of knowledge and good sense and a connection to Sayyiduna 'Ali (kw).
To Aminah Alptekin for giving me her precious time to turn a file into a book.
To Alia Nazeer for many readings and good advice.
To Fatima Sperling, and Dr. Munir Sperling for reading and support.
To Mahmoud Shelton for patient guidance within the mysteries.
To Bashir Saade for help in finding sources and hadith.
To Sayyid Mas'oud and family for information about, and pictures of the maqam of Yusha' (as) in Isfahan.
To Khalid Abulela and Ranya Hassanin for helpful comments.
To Radhia Shukrullah for being always willing to help with translations and good counsel.
And to the children who I hope one day will read it: Haniya, Humayra, Layka, Ishaq, Jacob, Hamza, Ghalib, Khalil, Noura, Karima, Tarik, Hala, Musa, and Yunus.

List of Abbreviations

(sas) – *salla Llahu 'alayhi wa s-sallam*. The peace and blessings of Allah be upon him. Prayer said after the mention of the name of the Prophet Muhammad (sas).

(as) – *'alayhi s-salam*. On him be peace. Prayer said after the mention of the name of a prophet or archangel.

(ra) – *radhia Llahu 'an*. May Allah be pleased with him. Prayer said when the name of a male companion or family member of the Prophet Muhammad (sas) or another prophet is mentioned.

(rah) – *radhia Llahu 'anha*. May Allah be pleased with her. Prayer said for a woman from the family or companions of the Prophet Muhammad (sas) or of earlier prophets when her name is mentioned.

(kw) – *karamu Llahu wajahu*. May Allah ennoble his face, a blessing given to 'Ali ibn Abi Talib after the battle of Uhud.

(q) – *qaddasu Llahu sirrahu*. May Allah sanctify his secret. Prayer said when the name of a saint is mentioned.

Table of Contents

Introduction: The Freedom to Serve...1
Map...8
1. Heavenly Roads...11
2. Finding the Light...19
3. The Birth of Yusha' (as)...27
4. Headlong into the Sea...33
5. Keeping Count...41
6. The Benefits of Patience...49
7. The Dangers of Pride..55
8. Two Blessed Men..61
9. Giants and Giant Slayers..69
10. Teaching Circles..77
11. Following the Fish...85
12. Mercy Oceans..93
13. Harun (as) Changing Worlds..101
14. Musa (as) Changing Worlds...107
15. From the Highest to the Lowest..113
16. The Commander of the Sun...121
17. The Lure of a Grain of Wheat..129
18. The Portion of the Sun...137
19. Some of the Secrets of Nun..145
20. Farewell..153
21. Maqams..161
Conclusion: The Middle Way..173
Postscript...187
Glossary...190
Bibliography..199
Picture Credits..207

We offered the trust to the heavens, and the earth, and the mountains; but they refused to bear it and were afraid of it; but mankind accepted it. He was always unjust and ignorant. (33:72). India, 1654.

Introduction:
The Freedom to Serve

The reality is that all created things are the slaves of the One to whom they owe their being and their becoming. **Whatever is in the heavens and earth belongs to Him, and those that are near Him are never too proud to serve Him, nor do they grow weary** (21:19). They have all, however, been given the opportunity to conform to their Lord's better judgment or to stand in opposition - **to come willing or unwilling** (41:11). There is no choice about whether to come or not. There is nowhere else to go. The only real choice is in the way to respond - with love and dignity, or kicking and screaming. To acquiesce willingly is to be a Muslim, one submitted to reality. This is the broad, all-inclusive definition of what it means to be Muslim.

All of creation, rocks, animals, plants, and even the earth herself, accepted immediately without hesitation to serve their Lord. They said, **"We come willingly"** (41:11), all except for men and jinn. They, in a manner of speaking, replied "We will think about it" and set out on a path called 'freedom' in order to discover if and when they might submit themselves to serve another. However, the way to be free is to give your service freely, not to be free of service.

When Adam (as) chose this way, creation shook in fear. **We offered the trust to the heavens, and the earth, and the mountains; but they refused to bear it and were afraid of it; but mankind accepted it. He was always unjust and ignorant** (33:72). As a result, man's journey through life on earth has become a test. Can we bear the trust for which we accepted responsibility? Can we hold on to the memory of the purpose for which we were made? The unfortunate answer was clear within a very short time. Adam (*'alayhi s-salam*) and Hawwa (*'alayha s-salam*) forgot and disobeyed almost immediately. To help us, the Creator has sent His chosen ones, people similar to ourselves except that they have not forgotten who is Lord and who is slave, who is One and who is many scattered pieces. The Prophet Muhammad (*salla Llahu 'alayhi wa sallam*) was told to say, "**I am only a man like you, to whom it has been revealed that your god is one God**" (18:110). Judging by its fruits, that understanding makes all the difference in the world.

First, Allah sent prophets with books and laws and stories. **In Yusuf and his brothers are symbols for those who seek** (12: 7). **Indeed, in the stories of these men there is a lesson for those who are endowed with insight** (12: 111). These are our guides, our models, our protecting friends. And He told us to follow them, they will lead to the path that leads straight to Him. **"If you love Allah, follow me, and Allah will love you and forgive you your sins; Allah is most Forgiving, most Merciful."** (3:31). Then He sent others to follow them until they form links in a beautiful chain that ascends by way of the Prophet (*salla Llahu 'alayhi wa sallam*) to nearness to Allah. We need to recognize the lives of the prophets as teaching stories and take them to heart.

What follows is the story of one of the prophets of Allah, Yusha' ibn Nun (*'alayhi s-salam*), known in English as Joshua. He is not only one of the chosen guides but, most importantly and uniquely, he is an example of what it means to reach that station by following another.

From early childhood he served tirelessly in the luminous shadow of one of Allah's greatest prophets, Musa (*'alayhi s-salam*) (Moses). Even in much of his own story, Yusha' (*'alayhi s-salam*) does not play the leading role. He is almost always second or even third because Harun (Aaron) (*'alayhi s-salam*) was there also serving quietly in the shadow of his brother. Yusha' (*'alayhi s-salam*) can be seen almost by the fact that he is unseen, silhouetted against the sun. And this is a description with which he would most likely be totally content and even pleased. It is not surprising then to find that one of the many resting places for Yusha' (*'alayhi s-salam*) is the place where it is said the earth spoke in reply to her Lord's question, to come willingly.

Allah Almighty protects and conceals His prophet Yusha' (*'alayhi s-salam*) even in The Holy Qur'an where He mentions Musa (*'alayhi s-salam*) one hundred and fifty-six times by name but the name of Yusha' (*'alayhi s-salam*), his disciple and inheritor, is not mentioned once. Yusha' (*'alayhi s-salam*), however, is referred to several times in The Qur'an depending on the interpreter. The most widely accepted references are in Suratu l-Kahf (18:60-62), where the Prophet Muhammad (*salla Llahu 'alayhi wa sallam*) informed us that Yusha' (*'alayhi s-salam*) is the servant (*fata*) of Musa (*'alayhi s-salam*), and then in Suratu l-Ma'ida (5:23), where he is one of the **Two men among the God-fearing whom Allah had blessed.** But he is also referred to more obliquely in Suratu l-Ahqaf, **"Have you considered: if the Qur'an was from Allah, and you disbelieved in it while a witness from the Children of Israel has testified to something similar and believed while you were arrogant?" Indeed, Allah does not guide the wrongdoing people** (46:10) and again in Suratu l-'Araf, **There is a group among the people of Musa who guide with truth, and who act justly according to it** (7:159). Some understand that the witness and one of the ones who guides with truth is Yusha' (*'alayhi s-salam*).

In the Holy Qur'an, Allah Almighty uses the story of Musa (*'alayhi s-salam*) more than any other as a vehicle for teaching. Many of the stories are related not once, but twice or even three times in more than thirty-four chapters. We need not be shy to tell these stories again or presume to think that we know them already. They reveal new levels of meaning to all who encounter them every time they encounter them. Much of the story of Yusha' (*'alayhi s-salam*) is actually the story of Musa (*'alayhi s-salam*), just told from a slightly different perspective. It serves as the sequel and the resolution. Yusha' (*'alayhi s-salam*) completes the mission of his mentor and brings it to, at least a temporary, happy ending.

It is clear that among the companions of the Prophet Muhammad (*salla Llahu 'alayhi wa sallam*) no one resembled Yusha' (*'alayhi s-salam*) as much as 'Ali ibn Abi Talib (*karramu Llahu wajhahu*). We offer one as comparison to the other for the purpose of familiarity.

The Prophet (*salla Llahu 'alayhi wa sallam*) himself, however, chose to compare Sayyiduna 'Ali (*karramu Llahu wajhahu*) to Harun (*'alayhi s-salam*). He said, "Is it not enough that you are to me as Harun was to Musa except there will be no prophet after me." (Sahih Muslim, Bukhari). Harun (*'alayhi s-salam*) stood by the side of Musa (*'alayhi s-salam*) throughout the whole of their joint mission. He was his support and his trusted companion. A prophet in his own right, he never took precedence over his younger brother and never competed for leadership. He, like Yusha' (*'alayhi s-salam*), was content in a supporting role. However, only the descendants of Harun (*'alayhi s-salam*) were allowed into the room in which the *Tabut*, the Ark of the Covenant, was kept. It was his sons who carried the prophetic inheritance, not those of Musa (*'alayhi s-salam*), and who constitute the priestly class in Judaism. Sayyiduna 'Ali (*karramu Llahu wajhahu*) was also given a special spiritual inheritance, attested to by his place at the root of all the lineages but one of the Sufi Tariqas. Most importantly, his descendants, the *Ahlu l-Bayt*, perpetuate the bloodline of the Prophet (*salla Llahu 'alayhi wa sallam*) and are accorded special respect by all Muslims.

However, in many ways Sayyiduna 'Ali (*karramu Llahu wajhahu*) had as much or more in common with Yusha' (*'alayhi s-salam*). They both accepted Islam as children and never wavered. They both served their prophets for most of their youth and were members of their household.

They were witness to the events of revelation which they related and recorded. As young men they served the prophets gallantly on the field of battle and were the pure champions of truth. They were left, after the passing of the prophets, entrusted with the task of guiding the community of believers. Sayyiduna Yusha' (*'alayhi s-salam*) led his people into the Holy Land. Sayyiduna 'Ali (*karramu Llahu wajhahu*) will accomplish this task in the sure future through his pure descendant Sayyiduna Muhammad al-Mahdi (*'alayhi s-salam*).

Yusha' (*'alayhi s-salam*) is not considered as one of the major prophets and his story is not known in much detail by Muslims. It has to be stitched together from bits and pieces of the whole cloth of the story of Musa (*'alayhi s-salam*). Out of a sort of misplaced jealousy for the preeminence of Musa (as), even the Jews regard Yusha' (*'alayhi s-salam*) as a minor prophet although he was responsible for bringing them home. As for Sayyiduna 'Ali (*karramu Llahu wajhahu*), in the last centuries the Sunni Muslims have pulled away from him in fear of appearing to be a party to political Shi'a or in fear of committing the excesses of Shi'ism. It could be said that his reality has been almost completely obscured by Sunni disregard and Shi'a exaggeration, with only the Sufis, perhaps, holding firmly to his true legacy. This is not how it was even in Ottoman times. Sayyiduna 'Ali (*karramu Llahu wajhahu*) is the prime exemplar of the teaching of Islam and of the way of the Prophet (*salla Llahu 'alayhi wa sallam*). The Prophet (*salla Llahu 'alayhi wa sallam*) said that love for Sayyiduna 'Ali (*karramu Llahu wajhahu*) saves from the fires of Hell. (Nisaburi). His is the path of devoted servanthood and heroic spirituality. Love for him is too precious a treasure to be discarded for any reason. The hope is that the comparison helps enlighten the natures of both remarkable men, allowing us to draw closer to them both, one by means of the other.

By his dedication to his master and devotion to his way, Yusha' (*'alayhi s-salam*) reached his station and completed his mission. He remained content in a supporting role until Allah called him to step forward and take up the banner. As the Prophet Muhammad (*salla Llahu 'alayhi wa sallam*) said about his cousin 'Ali ibn Abi Talib (*karramu Llahu wajhahu*), "I am the city of knowledge and 'Ali is its gate" so it is said about Musa (*'alayhi s-salam*) and his cousin Yusha' (*'alayhi s-salam*). When Musa (*'alayhi s-salam*) entered the Tabernacle to speak directly with Allah, Yusha' (*'alayhi s-salam*) prostrated at the entrance. But when Musa (*'alayhi s-salam*) left and returned to his home, Yusha' (*'alayhi s-salam*) remained (Exodus 33:11). In the reflected light of his teacher he grew to manhood, a model of honor and courage, of compassion and wisdom, of heroic manliness and, in the most exalted sense - of humanness.

This is the classic story of outrageous tyrants and the courageous men and women who, by serving their Creator, were given the authority to end the tyranny. This is also the story of the perfection of the path of master and disciple. It is no coincidence that it was Yusha' (*'alayhi s-salam*) who, the Prophet (*salla Llahu 'alayhi wa sallam*) told us, was Musa's (*'alayhi s-salam*) companion when he met with the ultimate teacher and guide, Sayyiduna al-Khidr (*'alayhi s-salam*). Every step of his life was a lesson in following. Yusha' (*'alayhi s-salam*) reached his goal by effort and imitation, obedience and service. He was given the opportunity and he chose the path which he followed without swerving right or left. He set his feet in the footprints of his master and he followed them all the way to the Promised Land.

In reliving the stories of these true heroes, in following their traces, *insha Allah* (God willing), they will guide all of us home.

Abu Simbel temple in Aswan built by Rameses II with no less than four colossal statues of himself at the entrance.

1.
Heavenly Roads

It was a dark time for the sons of the Prophet Ya'qub (as), known as the Banu Isra'il. They had entered the kingdom of Egypt three hundred years previously at the invitation of their brother, the prophet Yusuf (as). Their jealously over the favor he found with their father and their Lord had led them to try to kill him but Yusuf (as) had forgiven them and returned their cruelty with kindness. The king of Egypt had become Yusuf's (as) friend and a believer in Allah. He extended his welcome to Yusuf's (as) father, eleven brothers, and their families. Three hundred and thirteen men, with their women and children, had loaded their pack animals, rounded up their flocks, and moved from the drought-stricken hills of Canaan in search of greener pastures. Three hundred and thirteen men, with their women and children, left behind the land their Lord had promised to their great-grandfather Ibrahim (as), a land marked forever by the traces of his spiritual journey, for the grasses of Goshen in the Nile Delta. They were three hundred and thirteen men, with their women and children, the number of noble Messengers (*rusul*) Allah has sent to the world, the number of Muslims who fought beside the Prophet

Muhammad (sas) at Badr, the number of generals who will support the Mahdi (as) when his time arrives.

Over the course of three centuries, however, things change and, in this case, not for the better. What had begun as an invitation to shelter in a nation submitted to the rule of God, slowly became an enslavement to rulers who believed only in their own desires and their own divinity. The king became a pharaoh and declared himself a god. As his power increased, the welfare of the Banu Isra'il decreased. The pharaoh at this time, whom al-Tabari names Walid ibn Mus'ab and the majority of scholars have tentatively identified as Rameses II, had developed a personal dread and hatred of the Banu Isra'il. It is explained that he had had a dream in which he saw them multiplying like fruit and coming as a fire to consume his kingdom. The teenage Rameses had in fact mounted his first military campaign against the inhabitants of Canaan. It had failed ingloriously. He had lost face and almost his life. He never forgot this first major defeat and devoted much effort throughout his long reign to transform its memory, erecting fraudulent memorials to celebrate a victory that never really was. A builder by disposition, he continued to monumentalize himself throughout the land. Finally, he conceived of a clever plan. He would build a marvelous new capital city right in the heart of Goshen and conscript the resident Banu Isra'il to construct it for him.

Part of a frieze from Abu Simbel, Aswan, showing a young Rameses killing two bearded Canaanite warriors.

The children of Isra'il (as) were no longer honored guests nor were they even respected citizens. They were reduced to a class of laborer indentured to the state, only a little above the level of slaves. They were no longer free to move about the eastern delta to pasture their herds, nor were they free to conduct their lives as their prophets had instructed them, as their Creator had ordained for them. At every turn they were barred and bound. They were conscripted to build monuments to Pharaoh, objects of granite and marble whose major purpose was to defy time and God, the Owner of Time. The Pharaoh was no longer a good shepherd protecting and caring for the weakest of his people, rather he had become a despot. The weak were simply chattel to be worked until every bit of usefulness had been wrung out of them.

The children of Ya'qub (as) were the noble sons of prophets. They did not bend and bow easily to a worldly tyrant. The Pharaoh finally chose to eliminate the problem by eliminating them. **Pharaoh exalted himself in the land, and divided its people into factions. He persecuted a group of them, slaughtering their sons, while sparing their daughters. He was truly a corrupter** (28:4). He ordered the midwives of the land to report the birth of any male child to an Israelite mother and to have the infant killed and tossed into the River Nile. It is said that thousands of blameless baby boys were buried under the waves of a river whose source, according to hadith, is in Paradise.

Eventually Pharaoh's landlords and overseers started to complain because their work force was dying and there were no more boys to replenish it. So, Pharaoh repented and stopped killing the infant boys every year and just killed them every other year. In the face of this dehumanizing process the Banu Isra'il began to shut their eyes to a truth that was too hard to bear and they lost sight of who they had been created to be. The One Almighty God had chosen them above the worlds, to be His people. He had sent them messengers and prophets to teach them the ways in which life could be lived in fullness and fruitfulness, in a way pleasing to Him, in harmony with the purpose of their creation. However, they had let the dark shadow of the tyrant block the light of prophecy. They had begun to believe that perhaps there was no god other than Pharaoh, no recourse except to please him. They were slowly but surely forgetting Allah.

However, Allah the most Compassionate, the most Merciful had not forgotten them. Out of the miserable shacks and mental shackles of what remained of the noble and luminous descendants of prophets, Allah was preparing to raise up another radiant light. To a blessed family of believers, 'Imran (ra) and his wife Yuchabad (rah), were born three special children: Musa (as), Harun (as), and their sister Maryam (rah).

Maryam (rah) was a girl and so not threatened by Pharaoh's paranoia. Harun (as) was born in an off year when the boy babies were allowed to live. Musa (as), however, was born in a year of killing. His mother, strengthened by Allah, followed the inspiration sent down to her receptive heart. Relying on Allah's promise that He would bring him back to her, she put her beautiful infant son into a small coffin and set it adrift on the currents of the Nile. Her daughter, sent to keep watch, witnessed in horror as the small treasure-laden box swung into the canal that ran by the palace of Pharaoh. There, her heart racing in her chest, she watched as the queen drew him out of the water and onto her lap. Who could resist the beautiful smiling face of the radiant infant? Even Pharaoh for a second was drawn in and his hardened heart softened with the distant memory of kindness and compassion. Musa (as), the infant son of the Banu Isra'il, was adopted and sheltered in the home of his enemy. **And the family of Pharaoh took him up, that he might become for them an enemy and a**

Finding Musa (as). Rembrandt sketch (17th century).

source of grief. (28:8). In their hearts they knew the truth but since they did not acknowledge that the heart has a voice they proceeded to arrange for their own destruction.

Musa (as) was not permitted to take his sustenance from an unbeliever and so, as promised, Allah Almighty contrived to have him returned to his mother to be nursed. Growing up between the house of the oppressor and the home of the oppressed, it was clear to him on which side lay the truth and to which side he belonged. A member of the privileged by education, a member of the exploited by birth, a member of the truly elite by nature, Musa (as) grew to manhood under the eye of Allah. **And I spread My love over you that you might be raised under My eye.** (20:39).

One day he woke from his royal bed. It was a day of celebration and all the people had left the town to attend the festivities. As he walked the empty streets, Musa (as) saw a foreman of the Pharaoh beating a young man of the Banu Isra'il. Running over, he tried to protect the young man by pulling the aggressor away. Musa (as) was, after all, a member of the privileged class, as his dress and manner clearly signaled, a member of the Pharaoh's own household. He had a right, he felt, to interfere where there was injustice. In his attempt to separate the two combatants, he pushed the guard harder than he intended. Due to the power of truth that his right hand carried, the blow he struck for justice was lethal. Pharaoh's man fell lifeless to the ground. Musa (as) and the one he saved stepped back in horror. There were no other witnesses so Musa (as) returned to his home. Shaken and repentant, he waited for Allah's judgment. Nothing happened.

Next morning, he was walking in the city, fearful and vigilant, when suddenly the man he had helped the day before cried out to him for help. Musa said, 'You are clearly a troublemaker.' (28:18). Musa (as) realized that the one for whom he had committed unintentional manslaughter was not worthy of his protection. As the Prophet (sas) has said, "The most hated person in the sight of Allah is the most quarrelsome."

(Sahih Bukhari). "Truly the one who calls others to fight is an oppressive rebel *(baghi)*" ('Ali ibn Abi Talib (kw)). Musa (as) turned toward the man fiercely. Afraid for his own life this time, the young man said **"O Musa do you want to kill me today as you killed the other man yesterday?"** (28:19). In consequence he inadvertently betrayed Musa (as) to the gathering crowd. A little while later **a man came running from the furthest part of the city and said, "Musa, the authorities are talking about killing you, so leave - this is my sincere advice."** (28:20).

Musa (as) had no recourse other than to leave family, fortune, and future plans behind and flee for his life. He came face to face with the reality of his abject helplessness. He lay in the palm of Allah's hand, waiting for what would come. He prayed for forgiveness and vowed never again to act without heavenly guidance. He said, **"My Lord I have wronged my own soul. Forgive me... I will never again be a supporter of the guilty."** (28:16-17). And he was forgiven and he was guided.

He had woken up in the morning a prince and heir to one of the wealthiest kingdoms on earth. By evening he was a barefoot fugitive. He was forced to flee for his life through the trackless, barren wastes and across the sea to a foreign land. Musa (as) turned his back on the world and turned his face to Allah. He traded his inheritance for his destiny, and his material wealth for spiritual treasure. He said with hope and faith, **"Perhaps my Lord may guide me to the right road."** (28:22). Sayyiduna 'Ali (kw), in an effort to communicate something of his own reality, once said, "The roads of heaven are more familiar to me than those of earth." And so it was that Musa (as) began his journey onto heavenly roads.

Inside the Ben Ezra synagogue that is believed to have been built on the spot where Musa (as) was pulled from the Nile by the servants of Pharaoh. Cairo, Egypt.

Musa (as) sitting with Shu'ayb (as) and his two daughters, one of which would become his wife Saffura (rah). 16th century India.

2.
Finding the Light

Guided by Allah, Musa (as) arrived penitent and impoverished on a foreign shore. There he offered his service to two young women trying to water their sheep at a well overrun by men who were draining it dry to provide for their own large herds. This act of charity was rewarded with a spiritual opening and Musa (as) entered the family of Shu'ayb (as) (Jethro), the prophet of Madyan, as shepherd, disciple, and eventually son-in-law.

While Musa (as) was being prepared in exile in Madyan for his future role as prophet to his people, Harun (as), his older brother, continued to serve those people as best he could. He was a handsome, articulate, charismatic man totally submitted to his Lord and wise in so many ways. If he had any fault it was perhaps that he was too kind and forgiving. His sympathetic heart was prey to the excuses and wiles of others. He was a conciliator not a judge, a peacemaker not a warrior. He circulated among the tribes trying to settle disputes and bring people together. He recited the books Allah had sent their prophet ancestors, the book of Ibrahim (as), of Isma'il (as), the words of Ishaq (as), Ya'qub (as), and Yusuf (as). He related their lives and their stories. He tried to awaken in the people the remembrance of the promise they had made to obey their Creator, to worship Him alone and no other. Harun (as) was always welcomed with joy because the people loved him and he made them hope for a better future for themselves and their children, free from the tyranny of Pharaoh. But as much as they loved him, they did not believe him and he was not strong enough to help them resist the pull of the unbelieving society that engulfed them.

Harun (as) was not the only one vying for the hearts of the Banu Isra'il. There were others, like his cousin Qarun, who had a totally opposite plan to remedy their miserable existence under Pharaoh. Qarun had assimilated to Egyptian ways, worshipped Egyptian deities, dressed and lived in an Egyptian manner. By so doing he had managed to acquire wealth beyond measure. He used his money sparingly as gifts and charity to encourage his people to follow his example and to claim him as their leader. The young were dazzled, the old were jealous. They listened to him and aspired to be like him. **And he went out before his people in his splendor. Those who desired the worldly life said, "If only we possessed the likes of what Qarun was given. He is indeed a possessor of great good fortune."** (28:79).

Qarun was rich, he was fantastically rich. He paraded amid the poverty of his people in a golden chariot drawn by fine horses caparisoned in jewels. He was surrounded by retainers, handsome young men and women, whom he outfitted in matching robes of purple and gold. He presented quite the spectacle, the epitome of wealth and success. He was also an intimate of the Pharaoh, for evil enjoys its own company. Sometimes, but not often, he used his influence as a means of acquiring mercy for the suffering Banu Isra'il. With this show of pomp and power, it seemed like his way was the one to follow. What Harun (as), on the other hand, was offering was less immediate and less tangible: a future palace in Paradise, the love of an unseen God, and a heart at peace. Harun (as), having not yet attained to his future station as a prophet of God, was not able to entice the children of Isra'il back to the straight way, no matter how much they loved him.

There were a handful of people who maintained their belief in Allah and kept their covenant. They were steadfast, being generous in poverty, thankful in suffering. Among these few was a man we know only by the name of Nun (ra). The chroniclers generally collapse three hundred years into only three generations by saying Nun (ra) was a grandson of the prophet Yusuf (as) and his Egyptian wife Zulaykha (rah) through their son Ephraim. He was a contemporary of Musa (as) and Harun (as) and in fact a cousin since the prophets were the grandchildren of Yusuf's (as) half-brother Levi (as). Nun (ra) and Musa (as) were the grandchildren of brothers.

Whether he was a believer at birth or became a believer again under the influence of Harun (as) or Musa (as) we do not know. We have been given no information in any of the traditions about Nun (ra) himself. We can only assume that he was the kind of man for whom Allah had opened some of the mysteries of creation, a man who might have accompanied and supported Harun (as) in his rounds among the people. Although poor and disenfranchised, they set an example of what it meant to be rightly guided, to be clean and pure, to be shining with an inner light, the willing slaves, not of Pharaoh, but of Allah alone.

Nun is an unusual name that occurs nowhere else among the books of the Jews or Christians. According to Muslim scholars, it signifies in both Hebrew and Arabic either the fourteenth letter of the alphabet or the great fish upon whose back the universe rides. It has been suggested that perhaps Nun (ra) was born in a year in which Pharaoh was killing all the baby boys of the Banu Isra'il. He was thrown into the river to die but was caught like a fish and miraculously saved in the very same way that Musa (as) was fished out of the water. For this reason, he was called Nun (ra), fish. But there is another possible origin for this unique name.

The god Nun was the oldest of the gods of Egypt, although his worship at that time was mostly ignored or forgotten. He was the god of the void that, far from being empty, was the source of everything. He was the god of the unseen, of the dark seas that existed before the world as we know it, the source of the Nile, the source of life. The Egyptians, by the time of Musa (as), worshipped newer gods, Nun's supposed children, who were manifest in natural objects or human attributes. However, they continued to build a pool of water in front of every temple to represent Nun, the unseen god of precreation. Nun was perhaps the name that the prophet Yusuf (as) had chosen to call Allah in the language of Egypt, as we might say 'God' instead of Allah in order to show that He is One God by whatever name you call Him. **We have never sent a messenger who did not use his people's own language to make things clear for them.** (14:4). We do not know for sure what name the Banu Isra'il called Allah before the Tawrah revealed the unutterable name YHWH, the so-called Tetragrammaton, but Bible scholars think it was simply El Shaddai (God Almighty) or El Elyon (God Most High).

It is thought that the word *moses, meses,* is an Egyptian word meaning 'son of'. Rameses is a conjunction of Ra, the sun god, and *moses* which together mean, 'son of the sun'. The prophet Musa (as) had once had a conjunct name but the first part was dropped. So it could be that Nun (ra) had also had a conjunct name but the final part was dropped. As we might call 'Abdu l-Karim, just Karim or just 'Abdu.

Musa (as) stayed shepherding the flocks of Shu'ayb (as) in Madyan for ten years and then suddenly he felt inspired to take his wife and family back to his native land. Because he thought there was a price on his head, he must have only intended to visit his family there in secret, his mother Yuchabad (rah) and father 'Imran (ra), his sister Maryam (rah) and his brother Harun (as). There were others also he probably hoped to see - his foster mother Asiya the queen (rah) and perhaps his true friend, whom Allah mentions in Suratu l-Qisas, who had run across the city to warn him that his life was in danger. There were men and woman who had acted sincerely towards him and for whom he felt indebtedness and affection, men like Nun (ra).

On their way back across the desert of Sinai, a most remarkable event occurred. A storm arose in the rocky wastes, and the whirling sand and freezing winter winds blew the little family off course. Unable to see or travel, they sheltered from the storm. When it finally blew over they found they had lost the path and the live coal they carried to start fires had been extinguished.

Musa's (as) wife was about to give birth to their second son. They huddled together hungry and cold. Musa (as) looked anxiously in every direction hoping to see a landmark or a sign, much as Hajar (rah) had looked for water for her dying child in the desert of Mecca so many years before. Finally, Musa (as) saw something that appeared like a large fire glowing on the right side of a far mountain. **He said to his family, "Wait! I have seen a fire. I will bring you information from there, or an**

Verily! I am your Lord! So take off your sandals, you are in the sacred valley, Tuwa. (20:12). Byzantine mosaic from the monastery of St. Catherine, Sinai.

ember for you to warm yourselves." (28:29). Taking leave of his family, he headed towards the distant glow.

Instead of fire, however, Musa (as) found light. Allah Almighty addressed him out of the radiant tree in the blessed valley, **"O Musa, indeed I am Allah, Lord of the worlds."** (28:30) and instructed him, **"Go to Pharaoh, for he has truly become a tyrant."** (20:24). Musa (as) was ordered to return to the home of his youth but not in secret and not just to visit those from whom he hoped for welcome. He must return openly with a message to those who hated him and to the authorities who perhaps still wanted to kill him. He must remind Pharaoh of the straight way he had abandoned, the way of justice and compassion towards those put under his charge; the way of Yusuf (as) and Ibrahim (as); the way of the one and only Lord. Musa (as) was commanded to extend to his unloving foster father a chance to correct his ways and find salvation. Musa (as) in awe and humbleness asked his Lord to aid him with the eloquent voice and faithful support of his brother Harun (as). This was granted and the two were ordered to go together to Pharaoh and **speak to him gently so that he may remember or fear** (20:44). They were ordered to not antagonize him nor shame him but to approach him with kindness. And they were ordered to declare publicly that **"We are messengers from the Lord of the worlds"** (26:16) and to demand that Pharaoh **"Send with us the children of Isra'il"** (26:17).

The plant that is said to be the actual "burning bush" preserved in the monastery of St. Catherine at the foot of Mt. Sinai.

Musa (as) demonstrating his authority to Pharaoh and his men by his stick becoming a dragon. Behind him are his brother Harun (as) and the young man who would be his inheritor, Yusha' ibn Nun (as).

3.
The Birth of Yusha' (as)

The story of Pharaoh is a story of the proud, outrageous nature of mankind who, given a little earthly power, usurps the universe. And it is also the story of the patient kindness with which Allah Almighty responds until, out of His great mercy, He puts an end to man's tyranny.

It is not as if Musa (as) or Harun (as) were introducing a completely new concept. They were not told to inform Pharaoh of something he did not know. They were told to only remind him of what he had forgotten or rejected. Because **verily We have raised in every nation a messenger, saying: Serve Allah and shun false gods.** (16:36). Embedded within the profusion of the Egyptian pantheon of gods, and buried under the intellectual elaborations by means of which the human mind tried to make sense of them, there remained a solid kernel of the truth that Allah has sent to all people. The prophet Yusuf (as) had, in fact, come with a reminder only a few generations before. Of this reminder there was still some trace among the people of remembrance. Pharaoh had strayed far from the path of righteousness both as guardian and protector of his people and as deputy and servant of his Lord.

Musa (as) was occupied with the task of providing proof of his authority, performing miracle after miracle in an effort to awaken Pharaoh to what he already knew but was denying. Allah gave Musa (as) some special signs and powers to employ in his effort to turn Pharaoh from darkness. His right hand glowed with a white light like the moon. His shepherd's staff could manifest as an all-consuming dragon, and he was able to speak publicly without hesitation or fear. After many months of patient pursuit, Musa (as) and Harun (as) were granted an audience with Pharaoh. They made their way through the multi columned, elaborately painted halls of the great palace until they stood unbowed before the golden throne of an angry, arrogant king surrounded by his many contemptuous courtiers – two humble shepherds with God on their side.

Ridiculed by his foster father and challenged to produce a sign, Musa (as) threw his staff into the open space before the throne. In midair the stick spun itself into a fire-breathing serpent, whose sharp teeth, flecked with ravenous spume, threatened to consume the king, the throne, and the entire court. Pharaoh, momentarily awed, seemed to repent of his pride and assent to the clear evidence before him. But once the mighty dragon was sheathed back into the staff, Pharaoh recovered his arrogance and reverted to denial.

This was to be a sequence of events enacted over and over in the course of the full forty years Musa (as) and Harun (as) labored to reason with Pharaoh and his men. At one point, Pharaoh decided to organize a public spectacle for the purpose of discrediting the prophets. He invited them to pit their spiritual powers against the magical prowess of his court magicians. Pharaoh assembled all the best sorcerers of the land, the ones who contrived dramatic displays for the temples and festivals to impress the simple hearted. They knew how to make things seem to appear and disappear, how to make fireworks and smoky apparitions.

Pharaoh in his arrogance invited all the people to come watch the show. The sorcerers produced their cords and ropes which, by mechanical or chemical means, they made to wriggle and writhe as if they were alive. But when it was Musa's (as) turn, his heavenly staff took on its dragon form and summarily swallowed all the magicians' contrivances. The crowd was thrilled but terrified. They believed enough to run for their lives and even Pharaoh threw himself behind a barricade shivering in fear. The magicians, however, remained transfixed and stunned. They knew the difference between magic and reality. When they went to retrieve their cords, they found nothing. Apparitions do not eat objects. Their hearts submitted without further question or hesitation. They believed and ran only to take the hands of the prophets and testify to what they knew was truth. Pharaoh had them crucified, for this was not the truth for which he had given permission.

Musa (as) and Harun (as) continued to preach to the people and gather the faithful around them. They traveled among the dispersed encampments and small tent settlements where the pastoralist Banu Isra'il traditionally lived, telling people to worship Allah and be patient. Then Allah ordered a change. **We revealed to Musa and his brother: "Appoint houses for your people in Egypt and make your houses places of worship and establish the prayer and give good news to the believers!"** (10:87). Musa (as) was apparently instructed to encourage the believers to leave off their nomadic lifestyle and to settle in houses in the cities of Egypt. By living close together, they would find protection and they could also gather for communal prayer. By being settled in one area they would be prepared at a moment's notice for what they had been told was coming, their exit out of Egypt and their freedom.

Things continued to go on, however, as they had been before. There was no reprieve for the believers from Pharaoh's persecution. In fact, it may only have gotten worse. They complained to their prophets, **"We suffered hurt before you came to us, and since you have come to us"** (7:129). In consequence, not all the Banu Isra'il were ready to commit themselves to the guidance of their prophets. In fact, we are told that **none**

declared their belief in Musa, except some youths among his people, for fear that Pharaoh and his supporters would persecute them. (10:83). Many were reminded of the faith of their fathers and felt their hearts stir with belief but none were so sure that they would dare defy Pharaoh and declare themselves openly. They kept their thoughts to themselves and neither offered their support to their prophets nor to each other. Only a few declared their faith and support and put everything they had at the service of the prophets, men like Nun (ra).

On the other hand, not all the Egyptians were deaf to the truth. There were a scant few among them, exceptional men and women of conscience, who believed in Allah and His prophets. **A believing man from Pharaoh's family, who had concealed his faith** in the past, now **said** openly **"Are you going to kill a man for saying, 'My Lord is Allah,' and he has brought you clear proofs from your Lord?"** (40:28). 'Asiya (rah), the wife of Pharaoh and the adoptive mother of Musa (as), was a believer. Some say Pharaoh crucified her for her faith, but others say she miraculously escaped and found safety among the believers. Her handmaid was also a believer and, when Pharaoh discovered, he had her boiled in oil along with her five children. The Prophet (sas) has told us that he could smell the perfumed garden of their grave when he traveled high above it on his Night Journey.

It is said that the life of Musa (as) was composed of three periods, each of forty years duration. He spent thirty years growing to adulthood in Egypt and then ten years as a shepherd for Shu'ayb (as) in Madyan. He was forty when Allah spoke to him at the foot of the blessed mountain and sent him as His messenger back to Egypt. For the next forty years he struggled with Pharaoh and summoned the Children of Isra'il (as) to faith. The last forty years he would spend in the desert teaching his people until he returned to his Lord at the venerable age of one hundred and twenty.

When almost two-thirds of the second period of his life was over and he was still struggling in vain against the vanity of Pharaoh, something

Nabiyyu Llah Yusha' – Yusha' the prophet of God.

quite ordinary happened that received little attention at the time and no written mention. The unnamed wife of his companion Nun (ra) gave birth to a radiant baby boy in whom they could possibly already glimpse the signs of the fulfilment of God's promise. According to the Tawrah, the name they chose for their infant son was Hoshua' (as), 'salvation'.

Much later, after the meeting of Musa (as) with his Lord on Mount Sinai, Allah revealed for the first time His sacred name YHWH. At that time according to the Tawrah, Musa (as) changed the boy's name to Yehoshua', meaning "Allah (YHWH) is salvation". Yehoshua' was shortened and pronounced Yeshua', which in English became Joshua (as). This name change, however, is not mentioned within the Muslim tradition. In Arabic he is always simply called Yusha' (as). In the Greek translations of the Bible his name became Iesus from which the Arabs got 'Isa and the English, Jesus. The prophet 'Isa (as) was actually named after the earlier prophet Yusha' (as) and so, the names Jesus and Joshua, 'Isa and Yusha' are actually all the same name. They stem from the Hebrew root meaning to be unhampered, unfettered, free; saved from oppression and ultimately from death. It can be interpreted as meaning to cry out for help or to be the one who responds with help - the savior, the one who releases our bonds and leads us to freedom.

Crossing the Red Sea, by contemporary artist Yoram Ranaan.

4.
Headlong into the Sea

Musa (as) continued to demonstrate over and over again the strength of his spiritual authority but to no avail. At long last, Allah exhorted the earth to produce a series of natural disasters in an attempt to alert Pharaoh and his people to their mistakes and to warn of the consequences of ignoring their Creator. **They would say, whenever a punishment struck them, "O Musa, pray to your Lord for us by virtue of the promise He has made to you: if you relieve us of the punishment, we will believe in you and let the Children of Israel go."** (7:134).

First, came a drought that cracked the earth and desiccated the crops. The people repented but, when the rain returned, the people returned to disbelief. Second, came torrential rains that flooded the fields and reduced the houses to mud. The people repented but, when the water receded, the people's belief receded with it. Third, came clouds of locusts that devoured the new harvest and everything else. The people repented but, when the swarms retreated, they retreated into disbelief.

Fourth, came insects to pester and bite them. The people repented but, when they were relieved, they disbelieved again. Fifth, came the frogs to slime and disgust them. The people repented but, when the land was refreshed, they regressed. Sixth, the clean water of the Nile turned to red blood. The people repented but, when it was restored, they resorted to unbelief. Seventh, wild animals descended from the hills to savage their homes. The people repented but, when Allah recalled them, the people again ignored Him. Eighth, came the death of their domestic animals. The people repented but, when Allah revived them, the people again denied Him. Ninth, came a total and terrifying darkness. The people repented but, when the light returned, they chose to return to darkness. Whatever Allah did only increased Pharaoh and his people in stubbornness and denial. In his shameful arrogance **Pharaoh declared, "O chiefs! I know of no other god for you than myself** (28:38). **I am your god most high** (79:24) using the exact phrase the prophets were using for Allah, El Elyon. And it was written that **Those who believe, then disbelieve, then believe, then disbelieve, then increase in disbelief, Allah will not forgive them, nor will He guide them to a right way** (4:137).

During the trials of these last years, the believers were miraculously protected. Their gardens flowered and fruited, their animals thrived. They watched as their neighbors suffered famine and flood, death and disease, horror and terror. In compassion they poured water from their own jars to try to share their blessing but they could not avert Allah's judgment. The clean water that flowed out of the jars of the believers dropped in red clots into the cups of the unbelievers.

Yusha' (as) grew up during these trying years but he was young and perhaps did not notice much of the turmoil that surrounded him. He had been blessed by the prophets at birth and we can imagine that perhaps his first taste of earthly food had been a bit of date from the mouth of Musa (as), a practice of the Prophet Muhammad (sas). He stayed within their circle where everything was in its rightful place. As a baby he lay on his mother's lap listening to the rhythms of their prayer. When he was older, he sat on his father's shoulder as they walked the dusty roads following the prophets. When a little older, he made himself useful however he could, running errands, sweeping the courtyard, fetching water. Yusha' (as), like 'Ali ibn Abi Talib (kw), grew up enveloped in the sacred atmosphere of prophecy inhaling it with his every breath. Sayyiduna 'Ali (kw) once gave a Friday sermon in which he related something of his own childhood. He said, "When I was a child, he (the Prophet (sas)) took me under his wing… I would follow him as a baby camel follows in the steps of its mother. Every day he would raise up before me a sign of his noble character and encourage me to follow." He (kw) said, "I saw the light of revelation and I smelled the fragrance of prophecy." (Nahju l-Balagha).

So Yusha' (as) had no questions and no doubts because the truth was self-evident and the unseen palpable. He had only to trust and obey. When, after years of pleading and threatening, of patience and perseverance, Musa (as) was at long last commanded by Allah Almighty to abandon Pharaoh to his self-inflicted fate and to prepare the Banu Isra'il to exit Egypt, Yusha' (as) was more than eager to follow.

The children of Isra'il (as) were told to pack what belongings they could carry and make their preparations without alerting their neighbors. They were instructed to toast cracker bread on the flat stone hearths within their homes rather than to take dough to the public ovens to be baked. On the night before their planned departure they were told to make a sacrifice to God and smear some of the blood on the lintels of their doorways. As they huddled together waiting in the dark of their houses, they heard the wailing of a wild wind banging the shutters and making the palm trees shudder. It was the beating of the wings of the Angel of Death making his way from house to house on the command of his Lord. From each house that did not have the blood of sacrifice above its door, he took the first born of every living creature.

Unheard because of the loud lamentations and weeping of the unbelievers, the believers silently shouldered their possessions and left their homes to follow Allah and His prophets. They journeyed East in the direction the sun rises and towards the sea that separated them from their ancestral homeland. Their bags and bundles thumping against their backs or balanced precariously on their heads, they clutched their young and supported their elderly. They were organized in twelve groups according to which son of the twelve sons of Ya'qub (Isra'il) (as) they called grandfather. They moved slowly, a human stream making its way soundlessly, surely, to the sea.

They had already been traveling all night when Pharaoh was alerted to their exodus. He gathered his armies. Thousands of angry men, still mourning the deaths of their children, galloped on horseback or in horse-drawn chariots. They made up the gap quickly and the Banu Isra'il soon saw the dust raised by the hammering hooves and spinning wheels, like a black cloud looming behind them. The children of Isra'il (as) looked ahead of them and saw nothing but the rays of the rising sun blazing across a fathomless sea. They looked behind them and saw nothing but the glare of the sun glinting off the spears of their enemies. Allah had told Musa (as) **travel by night with My servants, then strike for them a dry path across the sea, and fear not to be overtaken, nor be dismayed. (20:77).** But they were both dismayed and fearful. **When the two groups saw each other, Musa's companions said, "Surely we are caught."** But **Musa replied** with firm confidence, **"No. Truly my Lord is with me. He will guide me." (26:61-2).**

The sea had been informed by its Lord of the task it would be asked to perform and it was anxious in anticipation. Its masses of water rolled one way and then the other nervously awaiting the command. Yusha' (as), however, could not wait. When the prophet Muhammad (sas) many centuries later invited the chiefs of Quraysh to belief in God, they remained stony and silent but Sayyiduna 'Ali (kw), only a boy of ten or thirteen, had rushed in to declare his Islam, indifferent to the consequences of their arrogant scorn. As Sayyiduna 'Ali (kw) said, "When truth was revealed to me I never doubted it." (Nahju l-Balagha). So Yusha' (as), young and impetuous, brave and confident, was bursting to attest to the truth of his master's word. He didn't wait to find out what the guidance would be or for a way to be opened through the sea. He leaped on his pony and rode headlong into the roiling waters. Almost immediately his gallant form was swallowed up by spray and foam and he disappeared from view.

Calling out in a resonant voice that could be heard even above the thunder of the pounding waves, Musa (as) respectfully addressed the agitated sea. "O Abu Khalid", he said, "O Father of Eternity, open a way for me." Then following Allah's command to **strike the sea with your staff** (26:63), Musa (as) raised his strong hands heavenward and brought the staff down firmly on the back of the sea. The mighty sea, in fear of its Lord and in obedience to His emissary, drew back its waters on two sides into mountainous heaves to reveal its sandy bed beneath. And there in the middle was Yusha' (as) on his prancing pony, alive and dry, waiting for his countrymen to catch him up.

This was the only time we know of in all of his long life that Yusha' (as) appears to have shown impatience. Perhaps the experience was sufficient for him to learn it lessons. Or perhaps it was not impatience that drove him headlong into the sea. Rather it was a sign of the bravery and sincerity that were to become his major attributes. Musa (as) was not too preoccupied to notice and take note.

Harun (as) led the children of Isra'il (as) safely through the tunnel of water to the other side while Musa (as), like a good shepherd, encouraged the stragglers from behind, and the Archangels patrolled the shores on heavenly steeds. Pharaoh pulled his black stallion to a rearing halt on a promontory above the miraculous scene. He tried to claim in his arrogance that the sea had parted just for him and, in hindsight, perhaps it had. His stallion, catching the scent of Jibra'il's (as) angelic mare, did not wait for a command but charged into the fray. The rest of the army had no choice but to follow. When the last of the oppressed had climbed out of the sea, and when the last of the oppressors had entered into it, Allah commanded the waters that towered over them to come crashing down. Each cascading wave caught an enemy in its curl and hurled him into its depths. Not one unbeliever reached the safety of the other side. All of them perished in the whirlpool of their pride. **And heaven and earth wept not for them, nor did they find respite.** (44:29).

Pharaoh and his men drown in the sea while Musa (as) and his young servant Yusha' (as) look on. Jami' al-Tawarikh by Rashid ud-din, 1305.

Jabal Musa, Mount Sinai, sunset.

5.
Keeping Count

Musa (as) had warned his people **"Perhaps your Lord will destroy your enemy, and make you successors to the land; then He will see how you behave."** (7:129). It was just ten hours since the dawning of the tenth day of the month of Muharram. The words of the prophet had so quickly come to pass. The captives were unbound; their enemies were gone. The wild sea of the night before lay calm and placid at their feet, lapping the shore like a well-fed cat. There was no one now controlling the children of Isra'il (as) but their loving Lord and their insatiable souls. They had been patient when tried with separation and deprivation. How would they fare when tried with closeness and favor?

The tribes settled themselves on the shore and began the process of recovery from their harrowing escape. They fasted in thankfulness to Allah for saving them from the hands of their enemies and then they ate in remembrance of the favors He had shown them. Excitedly, they related to each other, perhaps slightly exaggerated, stories of their adventures and exploits and they began to survey their surroundings and explore their prospects. However, there were already signs that trouble was brewing. It is not so easy to make the transition from slavery to freedom, from falsehood to truth. The children of Isra'il (as) looked around for someone to imitate, someone to follow. They couldn't help but notice that the local inhabitants worshipped some very nice idols, so similar to the familiar ones left behind. Shamelessly they scurried back to their prophet to ask if he could provide them with something of their own to idolize. Musa (as), impatient for his own reasons, had little tolerance left for this. In light of all the miracles that Allah had just bestowed on the Banu Isra'il, Musa (as) shot back a question of his own: **"Shall I seek for you a god other than Allah, when He has favored you above all creatures?"** (7:140).

Musa (as) dealt brusquely and, he thought decisively, with this nonsense. He had other concerns and he was anxious to be off. He told them over his shoulder as he left that he would be back in a month. Allah would question him later, **"Why did you come with such haste ahead of your people, O Musa?"** (20:83). Musa (as) excused himself saying, **"They are close on my heels, and I hastened to You, O my Lord, that You might be pleased."** (20:84). But it was he who ached for the promised meeting, for the bright mountain where many years before he had stood in intimate conversation with his Lord.

And Musa said to his brother Harun: "Take my place among my people, and be upright, and do not follow the way of the mischiefmakers." (7:142) Leaving Harun (as), with this very basic advice, to tend to the daily routine of the moving and setting up of tents and the constant complaints, Musa (as) set off across the trackless wastes, his heart bent on attaining the blessed valley and the sacred mount. He took with him, not one of his own strong sons nor one of his brother's, who would later be the priests of Isra'il. Instead Musa (as) took Yusha' (as) the young son of Nun (ra).

Whatever service there was to be done, whatever humble task, Yusha' (as) rushed to be useful. He didn't desire reward or praise. He was much too young to even know the meaning or care. He just knew that being close to the prophet of God was where he needed to be. Yusha' (as), once old enough to leave the lap of his mother, had clung to the side of the prophet. He had no interest in playmates or childish games, no social ambitions or spiritual aims to distract him. He could see the light in front of him and everything else was dim in comparison. Had Musa (as) wanted, he probably could not have rid himself of this singular child. But this he did not want. As it was Sayyiduna 'Ali (kw) who visited and brought supplies to the Prophet Muhammad (sas) in his seclusion in the cave on Mount Hira at the time of the first revelation, so it was Yusha' (as) who Musa (as) chose now as his sole companion.

Together Musa (as) and Yusha' (as) made their way along the sandy valleys and over the steep mountain passes of the Sinai until they came to the foot of the sacred mount. There Musa (as) left Yusha' (as) with their animals and supplies and told him to wait. His own eyes fixed on the clouded peak, Musa (as) removed his sandals and strode out over the jagged stones in his bare feet.

Musa (as) achieved the solitary summit that towers above its neighbors. No tree, no blade of grass, no wayward bird or lonely bee took shelter with him on that windswept rock. A ring of sun- or star- lit clouds hid the view of the ground below and the vast expanse of Allah's skies circled above. In this constrained but expansive place he entered into intimate seclusion with his Lord. Allah Almighty spoke to His servant out of an incandescent cloud, sometimes with a voice so gentle it made the stones moan with longing, sometimes with the voice of authority so commanding that the air crackled and sparked with tension. And it is said that Allah Almighty spoke to Musa (as) as one speaks to a friend (Exodus 33:11). Musa (as) fell to his knees, squeezed his eyes shut and pressed his face tightly against the hard earth as wave after wave of glory vibrated the air around him. For thirty days he never raised his head from the ground. The voice was more than enough.

For thirty days Musa (as) needed neither food nor water. As the Prophet Muhammad (sas) explained: "I am not like you. My Lord feeds me and gives me drink." (Sahih Muslim). Musa (as) remained in prostration for thirty days and was sustained on a spiritual feast. Although he had no doubt lost count of time, Allah **keeps a count of all things** (72:28) and He asked His servant to remain another ten days to make it a perfect forty. **We appointed for Musa thirty nights, then completed them with ten: the term set by his Lord of forty nights was thus fulfilled.** (7:142). What, after all, were ten more nights in the light of eternity?

For thirty days and thirty nights Musa (as) was trained and prepared in intense seclusion. For the last ten days he was taught the Law. On the last night, the fortieth night, he was taken on the wing of the Archangel Jibra'il (as) into the presence of Allah. There, still veiled by mist, he could hear the wings of the angels encircling the Throne and the scratching of the divine Pen (as) as it inscribed the Tawrah on tablets of precious stone. When he was returned to the mountain, the tablets remained with him as a gift and a sign for his people. They must abide by it, be true to it and not hide it. This was their covenant and this was their Law.

But Musa (as) was not yet ready to leave the realm of unity and return to the world of factions. In what was perhaps pushing the limits of familiarity, he begged Allah to give him sight, to let him see what, up till then, he had only heard. **"My Lord! Reveal Yourself to me so I may see You."** he pleaded out of longing. **Allah answered, "You cannot see Me!** And then in generosity and to demonstrate clearly to His prophet both his own and his Lord's reality, He said, "**I will reveal myself to the mountain** opposite you. **If it remains firm in its place, you will see Me."** But, **when his Lord revealed His Glory to the mountain, it crumbled to dust,** exploded into shards and jagged pieces, a testament to the unseen magnificence of its Lord. Musa (as) fell down senseless, not seeing or hearing anything.

When he recovered, he cried, "Glory be to You! I turn to You in repentance, humbled, forgive me. From now on **I am the first of the believers"** (7:143), of those whose faith in the unseen can be relied upon.

Gustave Doré (19th c.). Empyrean, the Divine Presence. Illustration for Dante's (14th c.) The Divine Comedy which, although very disrespectful to the Prophet (sas), is thought to have been inspired by the Mi'raj.

Humbled and appreciating the great gifts given him and understanding his own boundaries, Musa (as) was ready to return to his labor as messenger to the Banu Isra'il. When the Prophet Muhammad (sas), however, was invited to visit his Lord he approached with both sound and sight. He neither hid his eyes nor did he ask for more. **His sight never wavered, nor was it too bold,** (53:17).

Musa (as) had said to the people when he left, that in a month, after the wax and the wane of a single moon, he would return. The Banu Isra'il, as they moved slowly toward the sacred mountain, kept count: thirty glowing sunsets, thirty sparkling dawns, thirty starry nights and thirty sweltering afternoons. The days passed slowly. The nights weighed heavily. Musa (as) who spoke for them to God; Musa (as) who remembered what they had forgot; Musa (as) who replaced the bitter with the sweet; Musa (as) who had made them promises he had yet to keep - where was he?

Yusha' (as) at the base of the mountain also kept count. When Musa (as) did not return that night, nor the night after, nor the night after that, Yusha' (as) was worried but he did not leave his place or go to search for him. Musa (as) had taken nothing with him, not water or bread, not a cloak against the cold or a sheepskin for a bed. He had only taken the stick that Adam (as) had brought from Paradise, which had the power both to provide and protect. Yusha' (as) worried but he waited. Sometimes he could see the high clouds lit suddenly in an incandescent flash. Sometimes he could feel the air vibrate with the crash of thunder. Sometimes he thought he heard voices murmuring and sometimes it was as still as the hills around him where nothing was stirring. Yusha' (as) was frightened but he waited. Why should he worry, he thought, wasn't his master with Allah?

Jabal Musa at night.

Blessing of Joshua (as). Arnold Friberg 1953, commissioned by Cecil B. DeMille.

6.
The Benefits of Patience

When Musa (as) didn't appear after thirty days the Banu Isra'il gave up hope and stopped waiting. Maybe he had deserted them. Maybe his Lord had taken him. They were at a loss. But there were some among them who saw his absence as an opportunity to set their own plans in motion. One of them was Qarun who had inexplicably followed his fellow tribesmen out of Egypt. Perhaps he thought that with his material success and worldly experience he would easily outshine Musa (as) and become the king of the Banu Isra'il himself. Outwardly he accepted the authority of the prophets but inwardly he rejected them. He was always among the people questioning and gently mocking the actions and motives of Allah's messengers. He was careful but he was a hypocrite and, where he could, he whispered words of doubt.

The other was a man referred to in The Qur'an as as-Samiri. As-Samiri was not interested in political power or position like Qarun. Rather he was deceived into thinking that his own spiritual rank was higher and more inspired than that of the men Allah had chosen. He was convinced that he would be the best guide for the children of Isra'il (as) and that his understanding was what they should worship.

Shortly after Musa (as) left, the sea spat out the remains of Pharaoh and his demolished army. All along the shore, armor, weapons, and even whole chariots adorned with precious metals and all manner of jewels, washed up, tangled in reeds, to lie glittering in the sun. The Banu Isra'il could not resist the temptation to take the treasure and hide it among their meagre belongings. But to take the spoils of war was a forbidden thing. Anything pertaining to the enemies of Allah was not permissible to His worshippers. It belonged to Him and must be given in sacrifice. Not until the time of the Prophet Muhammad (sas) were the spoils of war allowed to be distributed to the needy among the victors. Harun (as) stood on the beach begging his people to come to their senses, to obey their God, and to behave properly. They tried to shut their ears to the truth of his words. Finally, their leaders, afraid of the consequences of displeasing the Almighty, convinced them to return what they had taken. Harun (as) ordered a big bonfire to be lit on the edge of the sea and for all the forbidden precious things to be thrown into it. The people obeyed. But as-Samiri, inspired by shaytan, had an idea.

At the time when Pharaoh was killing the boy babies, some mothers hid their infants in caves in the hills that bordered the Nile valley. Nursing them in the early morning and late at night, they left them during the daylight hours and prayed they would still be safe when they returned at dark. Unbeknownst to the mothers, angels would come and nurse these boys with heavenly milk in the interim. As-Samiri was one of these privileged infants. He was familiar with the company of angels and remembered childhood visions of angelic realms. He could see the Archangels and their horses when they came to help the tribes cross the sea. It had occurred to him to scoop up some of the dust trodden by the mare of Jibra'il (as), called the Horse of Life. "**I perceived what they perceived not, so I seized a handful from the footsteps of the messenger, and then threw it in. This is what my self proposed to me.**" (20:96). And now the same voice whispered in his ear again to throw that handful of

Golden statuette recovered from Byblos, Lebanon, 2700-2100 BCE.

dirt into the fire and pray for a golden god to emerge, something he remembered from his childhood visions.

When the fire cooled down there appeared the shape of a calf, a red gold, sleek and shiny cow just like as-Samiri remembered, just like some of the angelic forms he had glimpsed as a child. He was sure this was God and he announced with conviction, "**This is your god and the god of Musa, but he has forgotten.**" (20:88). "I remember what Musa (as) has forgotten, I know what he does not know. Follow me," he said. This was exactly what the children of Isra'il (as) had asked for, a little golden god of their own. And it was so perfect. Some say that the angelic dust gave the idol a semblance of life. It seemed to move and breathe and, when the wind blew through its emptiness, it lowed softly like a real calf. The people listened to as-Samiri and believed him because his conviction masqueraded as truth. They began to worship the calf, to give it gifts, to sing to it and dance around it, to touch it fondly and ask for guidance. They were far astray but had not Musa (as) himself asked for something he could see?

Yusha' (as) continued to await his master at the foot of the mountain. He was determined, whatever happened he would not leave the place his master had set him. He would wait an eternity if he must. He would remain there until his bones turned to dust. He quieted his mind and silenced his unhappy heart. He waited purposefully. Finally, on the forty-first dawn he thought he saw a shadow making its way slowly down the mountain. Squinting his eyes, hoping beyond hope, he at last recognized his beloved master striding indifferently over the sharp rocks by the dim light of the setting stars. He stood in greeting, his heart raced and perhaps even tears flooded his eyes. Of course, he always knew his master would return but, when he did, Yusha' (as) was so very glad to see him.

Together they retraced their steps back to the tribes. The tablets of the Tawrah were much too heavy for mortal men to carry so the Archangels again came to their assistance and bore much of the burden. Back across the now familiar wastes they walked; back to present to the chosen of Allah the generous gifts He had sent them.

But what did they find when they arrived? Definitely not what they expected, not even anything they could ever have imagined. The tribes were split into two groups ready for battle. One group led by Harun (as) was small but fierce, staunch and deadly serious. The other much larger group was cavorting drunken around a golden object beside which as-Samiri sanctimoniously stood. What a terrible shock for Musa (as) and his boy, coming as they did directly from the Divine Presence, carrying in their arms His gift, His Word, His Book. It took them several minutes to make sense of the scene that met their eyes, like men leaving a sunny courtyard to enter a dark room. When Musa's (as) astonishment and shock subsided, monumental anger rose to fill the void. In the fury of the moment all the power and strength that he embodied poured into his arms. Taking the tablets, which just a few moments before he could not lift, he now raised them high over his head and let them fall. They shattered in splintered shards against the stony ground.

It was done. Gone was the gift, gone was the grace, gone was the light. It is said that when the tablets broke, six out of seven of the letters written on them flew back to heaven. With the sickening sound, the moment also shattered and the people awoke as if from a bad dream. They were shocked into deathly silence and, looking around them, they were stunned by the depravity of what they saw. What had they done? What a terrible, irreparable loss. What an unconscionable disaster. Here was their beloved prophet, alive and well, bringing back for them the Word of the Almighty Lord as he had promised. And they? They had doubted and they had been unfaithful. They had utterly failed.

Their sunken eyes pleaded with their prophets. What was left for them? Had they lost both their here and their hereafter? Their repentance was late but sincere. Only As-Samiri, in his arrogance, like shaytan, was still convinced he was right. He was forced out of the community of believers to wander the earth dejected and rejected, repeating endlessly the sad warning, **"Touch me not"** - a spiritual leper (20:97). But still among the people, Qarun continued to whisper his insinuating doubts in the ears of anyone weak or kind enough to listen.

A strong and beautiful Moses with what remained of the tablets by his side, as imagined by Michelangelo (16th c.). After descending the mountain, the face of Musa (as) shone with a blinding light - *qeren* - rays (of light) in Hebrew which was mistranslated into Latin as *coronuto* – horns.

Jabal Musa in fog.

7.
The Dangers of Pride

What could be done now? What was the way forward and, more to the point, was there a way forward? Musa (as) approached his Lord and asked forgiveness for his people. Allah Almighty agreed to meet on the mountain with seventy of their purest and most honorable men. Musa (as) chose six men from each of the twelve tribes, seventy-two in all. Among them were Yusha' (as) and Kilab (ra) the husband of Maryam (rah), Musa's (as) sister. Kilab (ra) in Arabic, Hebrew, and ancient Egyptian means simply – dog. From ancient letters it is understood that a man seeking favor from the pharaoh would sign his name, "so-and-so, dog of pharaoh". As *'abd* is used in Arabic, dog was used in Egyptian to mean 'slave of', or humble servant. Allah, however, had only agreed to meet with seventy men, so Yusha' (as) and Kilab (ra), for the sake of peace, humbly offered to wait once more at the foot of the mountain.

The seventy (7:155) chosen were instructed to cleanse themselves and their clothing, and to fast. Then Musa (as) led them up the sacred mountain to the spot from which he addressed his Lord. A luminescent mist descended to envelope the prophet while the seventy looked on. Invited to approach closer they shuffled warily forward. Inside they could hear the sound of their prophet speaking to Allah. One voice was familiar and comforting while the other was royally commanding and relentlessly demanding. The unknowable, unimaginable, unfathomable Lord of all the worlds was laying down the Law in His voice of Magnificence. In fact, He laid down so many laws, including fifty prayers to be performed each and every day and two hundred and forty-seven prohibited things, that the hearts of these specially selected men rebelled rather than submitted. When the cloud lifted they forgot that they were there to beg forgiveness. Instead they presumed to ask that Allah make them all into prophets. Musa (as) humbly relayed their request to his Lord and it was granted.

It is related in the Tawrah that one day Yusha' (as), walking among the people, heard two men prophesying on their own, rather than in the name of Musa (as). In disapproval he sped to his master to insist that the men be stopped. Musa (as), far from being concerned, was instead upset with Yusha' (as). He said, "Are you then jealous for my sake? I wish", on the contrary, "that all the Lord's people were prophets and that the Lord would put His spirit upon them all!" (Numbers 11:29).

It wasn't enough that the seventy had witnessed their prophet and their Lord in sacred conversation, or that they had all been blessed with prophethood themselves. They also wanted to see Allah before their eyes. They did not accept that for certain things you need to be specially prepared. Proud and rebellious they tried to threaten Musa (as) **"We will not believe in you until we see the Lord plainly."** (2:55). Again, the cloud descended but this time it was less like a luminous mist and more like an angry tempest. All around them lightning flashed like sword blades and the thunder crashed in waves pounding their bodies until their hearts were afraid to beat. **Even while you gazed the lightning seized you.** (2:55). In terror they sucked one long last breath into their lungs which never found its way back out. When the cloud cleared, Musa (as) saw seventy of Isra'il's finest lying dead at his feet on the top of the mountain.

Musa (as) was devastated. These were the best of the children of Isra'il (as). These were the chiefs and the leaders. How could he manage the people or guide them without the help of these men? And what would their relatives say when Musa (as) returned with the news that all their elders were dead? But Allah knows what we do not. They were the best and yet even they had hidden in their hearts love for other than Allah. Musa (as) **prayed, "My Lord, if You had chosen to do so, You could have destroyed them long before this, and me too, so will You now destroy us for what the foolish among us have done? This is only a trial from You - through it, You cause whomever You will to stray and guide whomever You will - and You are our Protector, so forgive us and have mercy on us. You are the best of those who forgive.** (7:155). In answer to His prophet's distress, Allah Almighty returned breath to the seventy. He did so slowly, one at a time, so that they were witness to each other's death and revival. **Then We revived you after your death, so that you might be thankful**. (2:56). He revived them but He did not forgive them.

Allah Almighty told Musa (as) that the price of forgiveness was sacrifice. The innocent must kill the guilty, the clean must cut away the diseased. Death was the remedy for worship of other than Allah. **God does not forgive the worship of others beside Him - though He does forgive whomever He will for lesser sins - for whoever does this has gone far, far astray** (4:116). The judgment was that whoever willingly submitted himself to Allah's judgment would find salvation. The dead would receive the reward of martyrdom and the living, forgiveness. The tribes submitted to the Lord. Those who had worshipped the calf knelt on the ground with their heads bared and bowed. Those who had followed Harun (as) and remained faithful to their Lord picked up their swords. Allah sent a heavy fog to cover the scene. Led only by divine guidance, the truehearted sent to Allah's Mercy whomever their blades encountered. They could not see if it was their brother or father or son but they submitted their will to the will of Allah and did what He commanded be done.

The killing continued all day until the setting of the sun. Musa (as), Harun (as), the women and children stood to one side beseeching their Lord to forgive their men. Maybe Yusha' (as) stood by his master and prayed but more likely, like Sayyiduna 'Ali (kw), he obeyed by wielding his sword on the field of honor. When Allah Almighty lifted the fog, seventy thousand lay dead on the stony ground. Exhausted and dejected, the living begged that the rest be spared and Allah declared the sacrifice accepted.

With hardly enough men left to bury the dead, everyone helped in the task and the prophets led the rituals of mourning. Musa (as) lamented to his Lord that with so few men how were they now to establish His rule on earth. Allah consoled His prophet with the news that, at that very moment, the souls of the dead were being received by angels into Paradise because they had submitted to the will of their Lord and those, who had yet to die, would surely enter later because they had complied with the command of their Lord. All of them had found eternal bliss. Could the prophets have asked for a better end? And truly they could find no fault with the perfection of Allah's justice.

Musa (as) ordered that the calf of gold be ground down to dust because, unlike Harun (as), he knew that you cannot destroy gold by burning. The filings were thrown back into the sea from which they had come, the last polluted remnants of the tyranny of Pharaoh. Yusha' (as) had neither worshipped the calf, nor had he been struck down by lightning on the mountain. He was clean and clear of any association with the unfaithfulness of the Banu Isra'il. He had clung to the side of Musa (as), as his luminous shadow. He looked neither right nor left, not judging, not arguing, not complaining. He knew his place.

Musa (as) speaking to Allah on the mountain while seventy of the best of the Banu Isra'il lie dead at his feet. Jami' al-Tawarikh by Rashid ud-din, 1305.

"My people, enter the holy land which God has ordained for you—do not turn back or you will be the losers." (5:21). Afghanistan, 12th century Qur'an.

8.
Two Blessed Men

There remained in the possession of the Banu Isra'il two Tablets of the Tawrah that had either not broken when they were smashed to the ground by Musa (as) or that were given as a replacement for the ones that had broken. The shards of the original tablets made of heavenly gemstones had returned from where they had come. These were described as containing **the lesson to be drawn from all things and the explanation of all things** (7:145). The two Tablets that remained were carved into rough earthly stone **on which were inscribed guidance and mercy for those who stood in fear of their Lord** (7:154). Perhaps the difference in description reflects what was lost. What remained included the so-called Ten Commandments, a concise list of the actions that divert mankind from the path of God. A summary of these are contained in The Qur'an (6: 151-153).

Musa (as) was instructed to make a box to hold this sacred Book. The box was to be made of acacia wood and covered in gold inside and out. It was to have a lid and rings on each side through which poles would be inserted to enable it to be carried like a palanquin. The Tawrah claims that golden statues of two angels adorned the top even though the Banu Isra'il had just finished being punished for worshipping a golden statue. The Qur'an corrects this misunderstanding. The angels were not idols but actual angels. In The Qur'an it is called *al-Tabut*, the chest or coffin. **In it there will be tranquility (*sakina*) from your Lord and relics of the family of Musa and Harun, carried by the angels.** (2:248). Sayyiduna 'Ali (kw) described the *sakina* as like "a sweet breeze with a human face," a serene spiritual emanation of the Divine Presence, called the "in-dwelling" (*sakana*) of Allah.

They were instructed to house the *Tabut* in a small tent placed within a larger tent, both enclosed within a fence. It was from this *Tabut* that Allah addressed His people. Only Musa (as) and Harun (as) and his sons could enter the Holy of Holies where it was housed for fear of being consumed by fire. After their passing, only the high priest, a descendant of Harun (as) was allowed to enter once a year. Yusha' (as) had to remain behind a curtain but this did not deter him. The Tawrah tells us that Yusha' (as) sat in the Tabernacle close to the Tablets. There he devoted himself to studying the Tawrah under the direction of the prophets and pondering its wisdoms. Previously, he had remained by the side of Allah's prophet, now he made his place by the side of Allah's Book. Without wife or home, without employment or distraction, he devoted himself entirely to the Word of God. Like 'Ali ibn Abi Talib (kw), Yusha' (as) was both a soldier of God and a scholar, an unusual and, perhaps, an anguished mix.

The tribes regrouped themselves in twelve camps around the Tabernacle as the rays around the sun. They waited impatiently for what would come next. Finally, one day the divine silence was broken. The time had arrived to enter Canaan, the land they had been promised. They loaded up their wagons and animals and set out, led by the sons of Harun (as) carrying the *tabut*. They marched to the east bank of the Jordan River and camped just out of sight of the fortified city of Ariha (Jericho) 'the scented' on the opposite bank or some say Balqa. It was then that they discovered that the land promised them, what is now known as Israel, was not free for the taking. It was composed of many small independent city states at war among themselves. If the Banu Isra'il wanted the reward that Allah assured them was theirs, they would have to show they had enough faith in His word to fight for it.

Musa (as), as the commander in chief, appointed twelve men, one from each tribe, to scout out the situation. Among the twelve were both his brother-in-law Kilab (ra) and his trustworthy servant Yusha' (as). They set out across the Jordan River in the early morning and approached the well-fortified town of Ariha. Crawling out of the water they were spotted by one of the inhabitants, a giant by the name of 'Uj. 'Uj was the son of 'Anaq a daughter of Adam (as) and Hawwa (rah). She was the wife of Qabil (Cain) and she was an unbeliever. Allah had created the first men with heavenly proportions and great height. 'Uj, however, unlike his grandfather, was neither heavenly nor great - but he was big. He had been tricked by Nuh (as) into supplying all the timber needed to build the ark. At the last moment he had flung himself on the roof and so had survived the flood. He continued to live a mean and cranky existence for many thousands of years. He had met a lot of prophets and their followers in this time and had never liked one of them. Now looking up from his work he saw familiar little creatures climbing out of the water and he was both alarmed and curious. He strode over and scooped them up in his enormous hand even though they were not small themselves compared to the people of today. It is said that Musa (as) was ten meters tall and the grave mound for Yusha' (as) is seventeen meters. But to 'Uj's rheumy eyes they looked like bugs. They crawled desperately over his sweaty palm and between his filthy fingers trying to find a handhold so as not to plummet to the ground far below. The magnitude of his hand made them feel like grasshoppers (Numbers 13:33), a sensation to which these proud warriors, the chosen of God, were not accustomed.

Meanwhile, 'Uj was debating whether to squash them under his smelly feet or serve them to his chickens as a delicious treat. In the end, the decision was too much for him. He settled on taking them home to see what his wife advised because he knew she was a good deal meaner and

'Uj eating the fish. Zubdetu t-Teverih. Persia, 1321.

smarter than he. When she saw them, she did indeed have a crafty plan. She told him not to kill them but rather to send them back to their people so they could report what they had seen. They would inform their people how strong the giants were and how impenetrable their defenses. In this way the tiny pests would not return as a nuisance and an annoyance to the inhabitants of Canaan. 'Uj luckily thought that a most ingenious idea. He closed his gigantic fist carefully around the twelve bravest, strongest warriors of the Banu Isra'il and dumped them unceremoniously on the other side of the river, shooing them along with a wave of his massive hand. In a final gesture of power, 'Uj reached his arm into the depths of the river and grabbed a fish. Stretching his arm above his head, he held it so close to the sun that the fish sizzled and roasted. Then 'Uj plunged the smoking fish into his grinning, gaping mouth, chewing and chomping it menacingly.

The twelve scouts ran as fast as they could until they had reached a place of safety. There, unable to utter a word, they tried to catch their breath and regain their composure. Yusha' (as) was the first to speak. He strongly advised that they return to the camp quietly during the night and tell no one about what they had seen except the prophets. If the people heard about the fortified town and the size of the inhabitants, not one man among them would gird on his sword in the name of his Lord. The twelve solemnly swore to abide by his advice. Returning to the camp, Yusha' (as) and Kilab (ra) went directly to Musa (as) to report what they had seen. The other scouts went home. However, they were unable to keep silent about their terrifying adventure. Each one confided in someone else until even the dogs were howling in fear.

Yusha's (as) assessment had, of course, been correct. When Musa (as) and Harun (as) ordered the fighting men to assemble and prepare to march on Ariha, only two men appeared - Yusha' (as) and Kilab (ra). A general assembly was called and Musa (as) pleaded, **"My people, go into the holy land which Allah has ordained for you—do not turn back or you will be the losers."** (5:21). But the people replied to him defiantly, **"Musa, there is a fearsome people in this land. We will not go there until they leave. If they leave, then we will enter."** (5:22).

Yusha' (as) and Kilab (ra) alone spoke up in support of their prophet. They proposed a courageous plan demonstrating beyond doubt their trust and reliance on Allah. They discarded tactics of subterfuge or stealth. They advised marching straight up to the front gates and entering boldly. **Two men among the God-fearing whom Allah had blessed said, "Go in to them through the gate and if you do, you will be victorious. If you are true believers, put your trust in Allah."** (5:23). For their courage and their trust, Allah Almighty has rewarded His servants by recording for eternity His blessing on them and counting them among the God-fearing. The enemy perhaps was large but they were also stupid, overly confident, and cowardly. Allah would give the Banu Isra'il victory over them if they put their trust in Him. However, the people replied even more outrageously, **"Musa, we will never enter while they are still there, so you and your Lord go and fight, and we will sit here."** (5:24).

When the prophet Muhammad (sas) went out with the residents of Medina for their first encounter with the enemy, they did not find the caravan they had hoped for but instead faced a well-armed army three times their number. He turned to his men and asked humbly if they were willing to follow him into battle. When Miqdad ibnu l-Aswad (ra) replied, "We will not answer you like the Banu Isra'il answered their prophet. Rather we will fight beside you, on your right and on your left, before and behind you" the Prophet's (sas) eyes shone with happiness and he felt sympathy and sorrow for Musa (as) whose people had answered him so differently. And we can only imagine how much the loyalty and staunch devotion of Yusha' (as) and Kilab (ra) served to soothe and bring joy to the heart of the prophet Musa (as).

Certainly, Musa (as) was once more thoroughly fed up with his own people. He had suffered their rebelliousness and ungratefulness over and over again despite all he had done and all the clear miracles with which the Lord had supported him. At long last he turned to his Lord, his Friend and asked that he not be held responsible for his people's arrogance and disobedience. **He said, "Lord, I have authority over no one except myself and my brother: so distinguish between us and these disobedient people."** (5:25). And Allah Almighty replied to him that He would punish the Banu Isra'il by decreeing the promised land **"forbidden to them for forty years. They will wander aimlessly in the earth. So do not grieve over those who disobey."** (5:26). Those of the children of Isra'il (as), who had been led miraculously out of Egypt and who then refused to obey either their Lord or their prophets, would never enter the land they had been promised. All of the adult men who had refused to fight would die in the desert of Tih and be buried in its stony ground.

Even Musa (as) and Harun (as) would not live to see Allah's promise fulfilled. Only the little children who would be raised for forty years in the light of the revealed Book, under the eyes of their prophets, in obedience and faith - they would be the inheritors of Allah's promise. Of all the men alive at that time, only two - Yusha' (as) and Kilab (ra) - would ultimately enter into the land that Allah had promised to the descendants of Ibrahim (as).

Some say that Musa (as), Harun (as), Kilab (ra) and Yusha' (as) did, in fact, go alone at that time to enter the gates of Ariha under the protection of their Lord. It is said that Musa (as) himself ended the long nasty life of 'Uj ibn 'Anaq by his own hand. Musa (as) was ten meters tall and he jumped ten meters off the ground. Raising his ten-meter staff he thumped 'Uj on the ankle bone and killed him. But most agree that no one did battle that day or any other day for a full forty years. The death of 'Uj and the conquest of his city happened much later after the punishment of wandering in the desert concluded. Ibn Kisai reconciles both opinions by saying that Musa (as) and Yusha' (as) took Ariha together and expelled the giants but they could not occupy the city by themselves and so the giants returned. Ariha had to be conquered again later by Yusha' (as). There are two references to the event in The Qur'an that might support this understanding. The first is in Suratu l-Baqara where Allah Almighty tells them to **enter the town** (2:58). The second is in Suratu l-A'raf where He tells them instead to **dwell in the town** (7:161). Allah knows best.

Certainly, it is possible because Allah Almighty has said, **O Prophet, urge the believers to fight: if there are twenty of you who are steadfast, they will overcome two hundred, and a hundred of you, if steadfast, will overcome a thousand of the disbelievers, for they are people without understanding** (8:65).

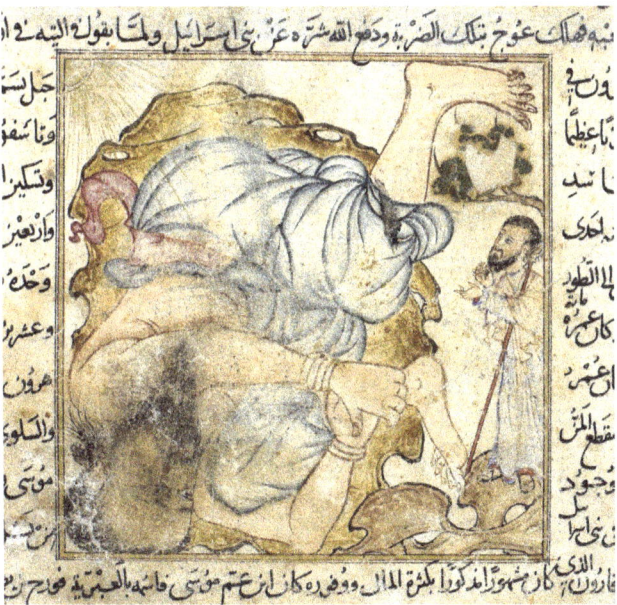

Musa (as) killing 'Uj. Jami' al-Tawarikh by Rashid ud-din, 1305.

Sayyiduna 'Ali (kw) using the gate of Khaybar as a shield. Persia 13th century.

9.
Giants and Giant Slayers

There was a man in Yemen, at the time of the Prophet Muhammad (sas) who lived alone with his widowed mother. His name was Uways al-Qarani (ra) and he was a herder of sheep. Only once did he receive permission from his mother to leave her and journey to Medina to meet the man whom he had heard was a prophet of Allah. But when he reached Medina, the Prophet (sas) was not there. Uways (ra), unable to prolong his absence from his mother, had to leave before the Prophet (sas) returned. Despite never meeting physically, in a very real but spiritual way, Uways (ra) knew the Prophet (sas) and the Prophet (sas) knew him. When he felt his death was approaching, the Prophet (sas) asked two of his most beloved companions, Sayyiduna 'Ali (kw) and Sayyiduna 'Umar (ra) to take a cloak he had worn and give it to Uways (ra) and to ask him to pray for the forgiveness of the Muslims (Sahih Muslim). They journeyed together to Yemen in search of him.

They found Uways (ra) on a hillside tending his sheep. Without turning around to look, Uways (ra) greeted them by name. At some point in their meeting he asked them a strange question: "Did you ever see the Prophet of God?" 'Umar (ra) took the question literally and answered that he had known him his whole life and had spent the last twenty years in his company. Sayyiduna 'Ali (kw), however, understood the question differently and answered, "Only once," although of course, he had grown up within the immediate family of the Prophet (sas) and had never left his side. "One time" he said "I saw the Prophet from the shoulder to the navel. Where his legs descended I could not see, where his head extended was beyond my sight." At this Uways (ra) nodded in assent. Allah describes this aspect of the Prophet (sas) in The Qur'an telling him, **you are of a tremendous nature** (68:4). There is a reflection of spiritual greatness in physical size that some can see and most cannot.

According to a hadith of the Prophet (sas), Adam (as) was created in Paradise in the image of his Creator and he was sixty cubits, around 30 meters, tall (Sahih Muslim). There is discussion, however, among the scholars whether or not when he came to earth he retained that heavenly height. The hadith goes on to say that the height of man continued to decrease after Adam (as). Musa (as) was said to be about a third of that height. The graves of the earlier prophets are extraordinarily long which is likely to reflect their eminence rather than their height. Adam's (as) grave in Muscat is the longest at 210 meters. The grave of Hawwa (rah) in Jedda is 120 meters long. The grave of Nuh (as) in Kerak, Jordan is 31 meters. Yusha's (as) grave in Turkey is 17 meters, while the one in Lebanon is 15 meters.

That those honored by Allah are portrayed larger than life is not hard to understand. They were men and women of immense value, gigantic stature. But there is also another kind of giant. These giants are big for different reasons. They are gross, overgrown, inflated. They are monsters, whose gigantic desires and huge appetites transgress God's laws and the rights of creation. They take up too much space, space that doesn't belong to them. As The Qur'an says, they transgress the boundaries and they cannot be contained. Their largeness is an affront to balance, to justice, to the rights of others, to the middle way. They take things too far beyond the borders of decency and humanity. They are ugly and dangerous. They are the *jabbarin*, the tyrants.

In the Hebrew Bible there are giants including the ones inhabiting Canaan. They are said to be the children of Cain and his sister, men and women who are inheritors of the first murder. They are not just forgetful or misguided, they are evil by intention. They are the human followers of shaytan, the proponents of lawlessness and chaos. Whatever is good, merciful and kind, they oppose. The flood of Nuh (as) was intended to clean them off the face of the earth but some survived, like 'Uj who clung to the roof of the ark. As a group they may continue to lurk in the dark places waiting to emerge, resurface, resurge. Sometimes they are portrayed as dragons and animal-like beasts because they have lost their human attributes. They will return in the last days as The Qur'an tells us: **when the wild beasts are gathered** in human habitations (81:5).

These two kinds of giants oppose each other in mortal combat for the souls of men. Now looking again at 'Uj we can see that it is not a humorous story about a grumpy old man, a Jack-in-the-beanstalk fairy tale. He represents an enemy of God who persisted in opposing His prophets and oppressing His creation in every generation from Adam (as) until the time of Musa (as) and probably beyond. When 'Uj speared a fish and held it up to barbeque on the sun it was, in fact, an act of murderous intent. 'Uj was threatening to skewer the prophets, symbolized by the fish of eternal life, Yusha' ibn Nun (as), and destroy them in the heat of the very thing they represent – the light. His evil power can reach into the highest ranks of closeness to God without fear or shame. He represents raw power without heavenly guidance. Yusha' (as) and the believers let him know quickly that they were not afraid of him or of his kind. They will march right up to his front door and face him down. With the help of Allah, they will be the ones to spear him and send him at last to roast in the fires of hell. It is interesting to note that Musa (as) is said to have killed 'Uj by hitting him on the ankle, *ka'b*, a word that derives from the same Arabic root as the Ka'ba, the join between heaven and earth.

Saint George (3rd century Anatolia), the Knights of the Round Table (6th century England), these are the champions of honor and belief familiar to the West. They kill the fire-breathing, treasure-hoarding, people-eating dragons. They release the innocent from oppression. They fight darkness with light, disorder with divine law, confusion with truth. And they win. These champions of courage and nobility are called *fata* (pl. *fityatun*) in Islam. Scholars have struggled to translate the word *fata*, into English. The most common rendering is the cumbersome phrase 'chivalrous youth'. To put it perhaps more plainly, a *fata* is a young man whose heart Allah has opened to Truth, who then mounts his horse (his ego), and challenges all the tyrants, both within and without, to fight to the death. Because he began his quest at such a young age, he has never sinned and then repented, never strayed and then returned. He is a spiritual warrior.

The *fata* is not just a champion of truth and justice, he is also one who pursues and eliminates injustice and falsehood with his only motive being to please God. The Prophet Muhammad (sas) identified two sorts of spiritual struggle, *jihad*: the lesser *jihad* which is a military struggle against an outward enemy and the greater *jihad* which is an inward battle against the self, its desires and delusions. When asked the meaning of fighting on the path of God, the Prophet (sas) answered, "it is to fight so that the Word of Allah is supreme." (Sahih Bukhari). Obedient, humble, patient, persevering, and brave; courageous and compassionate - these are the traits of the *fata*.

There are nine men whom Allah honors with this description in The Qur'an, two prophets and seven unidentified youths known as the Sleepers of the Cave (18:10). The first prophet is Ibrahim (as) who, while a very young man, took an axe to the idols and false gods of his people (21:60). He stood in opposition to Namrud, one of the first of the giant tyrants, *jabbar*. Namrud tried to kill him first by fire and, when that did not succeed, by battle. In the end, Namrud shot an arrow into the sky in an attempt to kill Allah Himself. He struck a fish that had been placed there by an angel. When the arrow fell back to earth bloodied, Namrud was triumphant in the belief that he had succeeded. But the blood of that fish became an army of tiny creatures that finally brought about his own miserable, ignoble end. The second prophet is Yusha' (as). He was given this title of *fata* at the time he and Musa (as) met al-Khidr (as) at the juncture of the two seas (18:60). Commonly translated simply as "servant" it, however, means more than that. He was, and would prove to be, Allah's champion, worthy of companionship with the most honored slaves of God.

To be a spiritual champion it is not necessary to fight the lesser *jihad*. The Seven Sleepers were young men who came to belief in Allah on their own and who dared to oppose the tyranny of their families and their ruler. Forced to flee for their lives, they took refuge in a cave. Allah caused them to fall into a deep state of unconsciousness for over three hundred years. When they awoke, all the unbelievers were gone and their people had become followers of the prophet 'Isa (as). **When you turn away from them and the things they worship other than Allah, betake yourselves to the Cave: Your Lord will shower His mercies on you and dispose of your affair with comfort and ease.** (18:16). They are called *fityatun* because of their youth, their truthfulness, and their complete trust in their Lord.

In the Muslim tradition, 'Ali ibn Abi Talib (kw) is the purest exemplar of *futuwwa*. It is said that a voice was heard over the din of battle at Uhud, saying "*la fata illa 'Ali*" – "there is no spiritual champion if not 'Ali" (al-Tabari). The young son of the Prophet's (sas) paternal uncle, Abu Talib (ra), he was raised from childhood within the household of Khadija (rah) and Muhammad (sas). At the age of ten he was one of the first people to accept the Prophet (sas) and he declared publicly his Islam when only a child of thirteen. He continued by the side of the Prophet (sas) all his life. He was a formidable warrior, winning every battle he participated in and all of the many single combats that were the traditional beginnings to Arab military encounters. He fought valiantly himself and, appointed by the Prophet (sas), he served as a brilliant commander on the field of battle.

During the siege of Khaybar, at a point where the victory of the Muslim army was halted, the Prophet (sas) announced, "Tomorrow I will give the standard to a man who loves Allah and His Messenger and whom Allah and His Messenger love. Allah will give us the victory at his hands; he is not one who turns back in flight." (Sahih Bukhari). All the companions hoped that that man would be themselves but the Prophet (sas) gave his large black banner, called 'the Eagle', to Sayyiduna 'Ali (kw). The next day 'Ali (kw) led the Muslim army through the gates of the fortress, to victory. His courage and strength on that day could be said to have been gigantic, almost otherworldly. He is reported to have ripped off the massive gate of the fortress and, holding it in one hand, wielded it like a shield.

Mawlana Jalalu d-Din Rumi tells us that during the Battle of Khandaq, while the Muslims and Meccans faced off across the trench, a Meccan challenged Sayyiduna 'Ali (kw) to single combat. They fought and 'Ali (kw) pinned his opponent to the ground and raised his sword to administer the final stroke. The man in defiance cursed him and spat in his face. Sayyiduna 'Ali (kw) sheathed his sword and walked off the field. The man was stunned. Later in captivity he asked why 'Ali (kw) had not killed him. Sayyiduna 'Ali (kw) replied that the man's words had made anger rise up inside him. If he had killed him at that moment he would have done so to assuage his anger, not in the service of Allah and His Prophet (sas). The man had never before seen or imagined such powerful control or such honorable behavior. He asked to be taken to the Prophet (sas) where he attested to the truth of *la ilaha illa Llah Muhammad Rasulu Llah*.

La fata ila 'Ali, la sayf ila Dhu l-Fiqar – There is no hero if not 'Ali, no sword if not Dhu l-Fiqar (the name of his famous double-bladed sword). Ottoman.

18th century miniature of Jibra'il (as) giving Musa (as) power over the earth to consume Qarun and all his household. Bibliotheque Nationale de France.

10.
Teaching Circles

The children of Isra'il (as) sat defiantly in their tents, watching out of the corners of their eyes as their prophets left accompanied by a handful of faithful. When the heat of their opposition cooled, they fell into the icy reality of regret. For another time they wished that they had listened and obeyed. As soon as the morning sun rose, they loaded their pack animals and set out in the direction they had seen Musa (as) leave the day before, hoping to catch up. They walked all day and into the night before they struck camp and slept. The next morning, they looked around and, to their astonishment, they were in the same place they had left the previous day. They packed up and set off again. The second morning, by the dim light of dawn, they could clearly see that, although they had surely walked a full day, they had gone nowhere. Their effort had resulted in nothing. They huddled in dead silence in the shade of their tents and waited for their prophets to return.

The prophets did return at last, tired and victorious. They had fulfilled the command of their Lord. They had breached the walls of the city of giants and killed 'Uj but they had neither the manpower nor the divine permission to do more than this. Although they were ready and committed to wiping out tyranny and establishing the rule of God on earth, this was not what Allah had written. It was time instead to step back and review their own situation. Musa (as) had asked Allah to judge the people and, once His judgement had been delivered, there was nothing more to be done other than obey. They had all been sentenced to wander in the dry rocky wastes of the borderlands, able to look only from a distance at the lush green promise that might have been theirs. There was a job to do before they could occupy this land that had been promised them. It was time to look at themselves deeply and engage in the greater *jihad*. It was time to besiege the tyrants within. They must raise and train a new generation to have reliance on God and to be obedient to His laws. It would be this generation who would reap the harvest, who would fulfil the destiny, who would enter the Promised Land in the name of Allah the most Merciful.

However, there were still some old problems that needed to be dealt with. Ever since leaving Egypt, Qarun, the cousin of the prophets, had continued to whisper doubts and insinuations among the believers. In a final move to take power, he paid an unmarried woman to claim that she was pregnant with Musa's (as) illegitimate child. Allah caused the unborn baby to speak and declare his true father. Only because of this miracle, not because of their faith, was Musa (as) cleared of sin in the ever-doubting eyes of his own people. After this, Musa (as) prayed against Qarun. Allah **caused the earth to swallow him and his house: he had no one to help him against Allah, nor could he defend himself.** (28:81). The material world that Qarun had valued above God and above truth, in the end literally consumed him. And it is said that, to this day, he continues to sink deeper into darkness.

Allah Almighty did not abandon His people to find their way alone in the desert and he did not punish them without purpose. He continued to watch over them, exhibiting in miraculous ways His love and concern in each moment of every day. They were never left to wander

The Israelites Passing through the Wilderness, Preceded by the Pillar of Light. William West, 19th century.

in the wilderness unguided. During the daylight hours, their migration was determined by a pillar of cloud. The believers packed their tents and possessions and followed the cloud in its circuitous route: first the cloud, then the *Tabut*, then the prophets of God and then the tribes. In the noontime heat, the pillar spread itself over them as a canopy to shade them from the oppressive sun. (2:57). At night they made camp by the light of a pillar of fire: the *Tabut* in the center within its own tents and fences, the people around it grouped by tribe. By the light of the fire they warmed themselves and they studied the Book.

Possibly something like manna on a tamarisk tree.

When they complained of thirst, Allah commanded Musa (as) to hit a rock with his staff and out gushed twelve springs, one for each of the twelve tribes. When they complained of hunger, Allah provided a white sticky substance (*manna*), that served as bread. It appeared in the morning like beads of dew on the branches of the sparse desert trees and on the ground. When they complained that they needed meat, Allah sent small fat birds (*salwa*) nestled in the sand outside their tents, waiting to be plucked and eaten. It is even said that, having no access to looms or markets, their clothes miraculously remained spotless and new. Babies were born with clothing and, as they grew, their clothes grew with them.

There certainly was no luxury and no excess. If they tried to save food for the next day it rotted or turned to dust. There was no cause for envy or competition, rivalry or ambition. There was no dependence on anyone other than Allah and no activity other than walking and worship. It was a simple life but full of goodness. Protected, as in the cupped hands of their Creator, they wandered for a generation, the time it took for all the rebellious adults to pass on and for the young to grow strong in body and faith.

Musa (as), who had most probably learned the art of writing as part of his princely education in Egypt, used this time to write down, on scrolls of papyrus or animal skin, the Tawrah, the Law. He copied the heavenly words imbedded in the stone tablets hidden in the *Tabut*. To these words he added the wisdom and understanding that Allah Almighty continued to verbally teach him. Yusha' (as) kept his eyes on his master and settled into the routine of daily migration and study. Most probably he helped Musa (as) however he could, carefully sharpening the pens to a fine point, grinding stones into powder to make ink, and preparing the skins or papyrus into scrolls. He watched intently as Musa (as) slowly and meticulously transcribed the words of the Lord and he probably learned to read and write as well. As his master's pen scratched across the scroll, each letter and each word were also inscribed on the heart of Yusha' (as). Each day he witnessed their meaning come to life in the actions and manners of the prophets. His heart was saturated with the Book, until it became an integral part of who he was.

The rock from which flowed 12 sources of water. Wadi al-Lija, Sinai.

In much the same way Sayyiduna 'Ali (kw) experienced The Qur'an. Word by word, *ayah* by *ayah*, light by light, he received from the mouth and the hand of the man to whom it was addressed. It began on the mountain where it was first revealed and continued to the oasis where the revelation was sealed. The Prophet Muhammad (sas) said that "'Ali is with The Qur'an and The Qur'an is with 'Ali." (Sahih Muslim). Sayyiduna 'Ali (kw) himself said that there was no *ayah* of The Qur'an whose provenance (*tanzil*) he did not know because he was witness to its revelation and of whose meanings, both apparent and hidden (*ta'wil*), he was not aware. (Nahju l-Balagha). The Prophet (sas) was protected by Allah from the ability to read or write in order to ensure no one could raise doubts about the source of his inspiration. 'Ali (kw) was one of the hands by means of which the revelation was written from the beginning until the end.

Allah punishes His creation, not to hurt them, but to teach them. However, first they have to accept that they are in need of being taught and then they have to learn how to learn. These were the lessons the Lord seemed intent upon teaching the Banu Isra'il while they were secluded forty years in the desert of Tih. It would be a long, hard road ahead.

One afternoon, according to a hadith of the Prophet Muhammad (sas), Musa (as) was teaching a gathering of Banu Isra'il. At the end, someone asked, in awe, if it was possible that there was anyone else in all the world who had as much knowledge as he. In all humility Musa (as) answered that he thought it was unlikely. Allah heard this statement of His prophet and was not pleased. Musa (as) had forgotten to acknowledge that only Allah knows both the extent of His knowledge and what portion He has granted His servants. No one can compass the knowledge of the Lord of the worlds, neither give it limits, nor quantify it. No one can know the expanse of His creation and what gifts He has seen fit to give each of them. You can only know what Allah has opened for you and that, for sure, there is knowledge beyond your own. **Above every knower there is another more knowing** (12:76). So, Allah told His prophet about the existence of another of His slaves, to whom He had given a kind of knowledge of which Musa (as) was ignorant. Musa (as) was not upset or angry to be reprimanded by his Lord. Rather he was determined to find this wise man and to learn from him. He asked where he could be found and was told to seek him at the place **where the two seas meet** (18:60).

Many have speculated as to where on the globe to find the junction of these two seas. Some say it is at the tip of the Sinai where the Red Sea splits in two. Some say Yemen or Oman where the Arabian Sea divides into the Red Sea or the Persian Gulf. Some say Gibraltar or Morocco where the Mediterranean meets the Atlantic. Some say the juncture of the White and the Blue Nile since the word *bahr* can mean any large body of water. Others say where the Bosporus drains the Black Sea, or the Shatt al-'Arab where the Tigris and Euphrates meet. Or perhaps it could have been somewhere near the Holy Land, where the Jordan River meets the Dead Sea. There are two events sometimes included in this story that suggest that at least one of the bodies of water was fresh and potable. They saw a bird drinking and al-Khidr (as) said that the tiny drop hanging from its beak was like their knowledge compared to the oceans of Allah's knowledge. It has also been related that Yusha' (as) drank and it was, in fact, the water of life (al-Tabari). Allah knows best.

Even if the destination had a specific geographical location, the event occurred simultaneously on a spiritual plane. The place where the seas meet can be explained as a metaphor whose purpose is to give substance to the unseen. So, al-Khidr (as) is said to dwell on an island where the great oceans, which enwrap the globe, meet. It is a place on the 'other side' of the earth where two known entities invisibly merge and become one.

The shaykhs tell us that Allah was referring to two oceans of knowledge rather than of water, in this case exoteric knowledge as opposed to esoteric knowledge; knowledge gained by the intellectual perception of reproducible events and the logical investigation of their physical causes, as opposed to knowledge granted by spiritual inspiration of the real meanings of events and their divine purposes. One does not occlude or exclude the other. They both exist at the same time on different levels of reality, as taste and touch coexist, as thought and experience coexist, as you and I coexist. But one is acquired by asking questions and studying the answers while the other is a gift either preordained, or earned by determined preparation in the critical sciences of silence, awareness, patience, and submission.

Suratu l-Kahf (18:57-63). India. Smithsonian Museum of Asian Art.

11.
Following the Fish

Musa said to his (*fata*) **servant,** Yusha' (as), **"I will not rest until I reach the place where the two seas meet, even if it takes me ages!"** (18:60). So Yusha' (as) quickly prepared what was necessary for traveling an indefinite period of time. He put a few day's food and water in a basket to sustain them for the first part of their journey. They were told, in particular, to pack a dried and salted fish. This would inexplicably be for them a sign. Musa (as) was anxious to be on his way so Yusha' (as), as ever the obedient servant, prepared as best he could for a journey about whose purpose and destination he did not ask and was not told. The only instruction he received was to keep his eyes on the fish.

They left the desert encampment of the Banu Isra'il and headed for Egypt, or Yemen, or Morocco, or Sudan, or Jerusalem, or a place not of this earth at all but of the heart. It was to be a journey in search of knowledge as the hadith prescribes. "To seek knowledge is obligatory for every Muslim" (Ibn Majah) and as Allah instructs the Prophet (sas) in The Qur'an to pray, **"My Lord, increase me in knowledge"** (20:114).

Seeking the pleasure of Allah and closeness to Him carries its own blessing and so they found the journey neither tiring nor difficult. Eventually they arrived at a wide body of water. They settled down to rest on a large flat rock. While Musa (as) slept, Yusha' (as) sat guard. He must have been very sleepy because something exceedingly strange happened whose significance he did not seem to fully appreciate at the time. The dead fish suddenly wriggled out of the basket and dove into the sea where it swam away through the water **in a marvelous way** (18:63). **But when they reached the point where the two seas meet, they forgot their fish, and it took its way into the sea, as if through a tunnel** (18:61). The dry salted fish, probably already partially eaten, became alive, escaped its basket, leaped into the water and, as the Prophet Muhammad (sas) demonstrated by arching his two hands into a circle, burrowed swiftly through the water as if in a tunnel. It was not just remarkable because the dead fish became alive but also because the fish, perhaps, swam upstream or against the tide, quickly without effort. Allah not only enlivened their lunch but stilled the current of the water to allow the resurrected fish to make its way back to the source unhampered. Surely this was a powerful sign for Musa (as) and his boy (as).

The word for fish in this case is not *nun* but rather *hut*. This word is not usually used for a small edible fish. For most of the Arabic speaking world it indicates a very large fish or whale. It is a *hut* that swallowed the prophet Yunus (as) (Jonah) and kept him alive in its stomach for forty days. When Yunus (as) tried to escape from the orders of his Lord and from his own destiny, Allah Almighty caught him in the mouth of His servant the *hut*. Yunus (as) is called in The Qur'an both **Dhu l-Nun** (Master of the Nun 21:87) and **al-*Sahibu l-Hut*** (the Companion of the fish 68:48). Yunus (as) experienced something like the inverse of the Night Journey of the Prophet Muhammad (sas), who was taken into the outer realms of light on the back of the *buraq*, a celestial steed. Yunus (as) was taken into the interior realms of darkness inside the belly of the great fish.

The fish was their sign but they both forgot. Musa (as) slept and when he woke he was impatient to keep moving. He forgot all about checking on the fish. Yusha' (as) was the sole witness but he, inexplicably, forgot to mention it. **And verily We made a covenant of old with Adam, but he forgot, and We found in him no firm resolve**. (20:115). Man is ever forgetful. Even the word for mankind in Arabic, *insan*, is derived from the root meaning to forget. That is why Allah provides so many reminders. We are told in The Qur'an over three hundred times to remind and to remember and The Qur'an itself is called The Reminder (*Al-Dhikr*). We were born knowing all this, how is it that we forgot? The answer is simple, if not commendable. We get busy with other things and other thoughts. The awareness of the presence of our Lord slips from our minds like the fish from the basket.

Waking from sleep, Musa (as) was anxious to get on with their journey but it no longer flowed effortlessly. Their travelling became difficult and unblessed, like moving upstream. The prophet and his companion began to feel the weight of it. Musa (as) stopped, thinking that rest and a little food might restore their energy. **And when they had gone further, he said to his servant (*fata*): "Bring us our breakfast. Verily we have found fatigue in this our journey."** (18:62). He asked Yusha' (as) to take out the fish for them to eat. Then and only then, did Yusha' (as) remember that the fish was gone because it had come alive, leapt into the sea, and swum away. **He said: "Did you see, when we took refuge on the rock? I forgot the fish and none but satan caused me to forget to mention it. It took its way into the sea in a marvelous way."** (18:63).

This was the sign for which they had been searching. The man they were seeking was to be found back at the rock. They had exceeded their mark. What they were looking for was behind them and that is why the day's journey had, for the first time, felt heavy. Musa (as) said, **"This is what we were seeking." And so they turned back retracing their steps.** (18:64) until they reached the rock a second time.

Near the rock they found a figure wrapped in his cloak waiting for them. **Then found they one of Our slaves, unto whom We had given mercy (*rahma*) from Ourself, and whom We had taught knowledge from**

Our Presence. (18:65). This man, according to hadith, is a mysterious saint or prophet called by the Prophet Muhammad (sas), al-Khidr (as), the Green Man, because "he sat on a white wasteland which became green after his sitting there" (Sahih Bukhari). If he passes across barren dunes or even a field of snow, he leaves a trail of greenery behind him. This is understood to mean that al-Khidr (as) has the power to quicken the dead - in this case the fish but, in general, the heart. *Rahma* is the word by which our Lord chooses to identify Himself: *Ar-Rahman, Ar-Rahim*, the most Compassionate, the most Merciful. In Arabic the word can be used for both compassion and for rain. Since it stems from the root meaning 'womb' it carries the implication of a mother's love, a nurturing kindness, as well as birth and rebirth, the regeneration of man and of earth. That is one reason why the resurrection of the fish was a particular sign of the presence of al-Khidr (as). Having tasted of the waters of life, he is not immortal but will continue to live and serve his Lord until the coming of Sayyiduna al-Mahdi (as) and Sayyiduna 'Isa (as). At that time, he will give up his life to save others from the Arch Deceiver, the Antichrist, known as the Dajjal.

Al-Khidr (as) knew Musa (as) immediately as the prophet of the Banu Isra'il and the bearer of the Tawrah. He knew the honor and high degree of Allah's messenger and he also knew his particular characteristics and even his limitations. When Musa (as) asked him humbly, **"May I follow you so that you can teach me some of the right guidance you have been taught?"** (18:66), al-Khidr (as) replied gently but firmly, **"You will not be able to bear with me patiently. How could you be patient in matters beyond your knowledge?"** (18:67-68). According to hadith, al-Khidr (as) continued, "Is it not sufficient for you that the Tawrah is in your hands and that divine inspiration comes to you, O Musa?" (Sahih Bukhari). But Musa (as) had been directed to this meeting by Allah. There was no way he would not persevere to the best of his ability. **Musa said, "God willing, you will find me patient. I will not disobey you in any way."** (18:69). He said 'God willing' when pledging to be patient but he failed to repeat it when promising obedience. Al-Khidr (as) further stipulated, **"If you follow me then, do not ask me about anything I do**

The meeting between Musa (as), Khidr (as) and Yusha' (as). Qisasu l-Anbiya by Nisaburi. Persian ca. 1850. N.Y. Public Library.

before I mention it to you myself." (18:70). And so, the contract between the two chosen men of God was sealed in the presence of Yusha' (as). Although the main actors were the prophets Musa (as) and al-Khidr (as), Yusha' (as) as witness was the silent but necessary third.

The Qur'an now tells us that, **the two of them traveled on.** (18:71). The use of the verb 'to travel' in the dual form is usually assumed to mean that only two people set out together past this point. Yusha' (as) did not join Musa (as) and al-Khidr (as) on their journey of companionship. We can only suppose that, as a young man, he was not sent to travel home alone but that he was again told to wait patiently by the rock, as he had waited at the foot of the mountain, as he had waited in the tent, for his master's eventual return, a paragon of patience. Yusha' (as) was left behind but being left behind in spiritual matters does not imply being left out. There is reward in accepting willingly to be in the place where Allah wants you. When the Prophet (sas) fled Mecca for Medina with Abu Bakr (ra), he left 'Ali ibn Abi Talib (kw), his young cousin, behind to lie in his bed and deceive their enemies. Sayyiduna 'Ali (kw) obeyed without fear for his own life or question about being left behind. Abu Bakr (ra) received his spiritual reward for traveling with the Prophet (sas) and Sayyiduna 'Ali (kw) received his for staying behind.

In a similar vein, the hadith scholar and sufi, Hakim al-Tirmidhi (q) (d.869), as a young student, was not able in good conscience to leave his elderly mother alone. It broke his heart but he did not accompany his friends to seek education in the centers of learning. He was rewarded for his choice by being taught the highest knowledge directly from Sayyiduna al-Khidr (as) every night right on the roof of his mother's house.

Three fish, one eye. The symbols of the sun and the fish. A Javanese, Indonesian illustration for a mystical text of the Shattariyyah Tariqa, 1790.

"Did I not tell you that you would never be able to bear with me patiently?" "Forgive me for forgetting. Do not make it too hard for me to follow you." (18:72 -73). Chinese Ming Dynasty (1368-1644) Qur'an.

12.
Mercy Oceans

Musa (as) and al-Khidr (as) looked for a way to cross the sea or river. A boatman saw them on the bank and, being familiar with al-Khidr (as), offered them a ride free of charge. Yusha' (as) stood silently on the shore and watched as his master sailed away. While the boatman carried them across the river, al-Khidr secretly made a hole in the hull of the craft. Musa (as) was understandably horrified. And he expressed his disapproval in the way he was accustomed, with the voice of judgment. **"How could you make a hole in it? Do you want to drown its passengers? What a terrible thing to do!"** (18:71). And so, he unintentionally broke his agreement with his guide almost immediately. Al-Khidr (as) reminded him, **"Did I not tell you that you would never be able to bear with me patiently?"** (18:72). Musa (as) pleaded humbly with him, **"Forgive me for forgetting. Do not make it too hard for me to follow you."** (18:73).

They continued their journey until, passing through a town, they saw some boys playing in the road. Al-Khidr (as) approached the most handsome of them and killed him on the spot. Musa (as) was understandably shocked and upset. Unable to contain himself he cried out again in judgment, **"How could you kill an innocent person? He has not killed anyone! What a terrible thing to do!"** (18:74). Again, patiently al-Khidr (as) rebuked him, **"Did I not tell you that you would never be able to bear with me patiently?"** (18:75). Musa (as) was forced to remember his promise and he asked for one more chance. **"If I ask you anything after this, keep me not in your company, you have received an excuse from me."** (18:76). He regretted having spoken his mind but perhaps still believed that what he said was right.

They continued their journey in silence. **Then, when they came to a town and asked the inhabitants for food but were refused hospitality, they saw a wall there that was on the point of falling down.** Al-Khidr (as) got to work mixing the mud, lifting the stones back into place, in order to right the wall. It was heavy labor especially when they were hungry, thirsty, and tired. This time Musa (as) perhaps did not forget, and did not speak out of surprise or horror. Rather he spoke out of frustration and fatigue. **"If you had wished you could have taken payment for doing that."** (18:77). Three mistakes, the journey was ended. It must have been clear to the both of them that their companionship had concluded. But al-Khidr (as) offered to teach his companion the wisdom behind his inscrutable actions. **He said, 'This is where you and I part company. I will tell you the meaning of the things you could not bear with patiently."** (18:78).

Then Allah relates to us the explanation for al-Khidr's (as) strange behavior. It turns out not to be so strange or irrational after all. It was in fact quite logical except that it was based on information that no one other than al-Khidr (as) possessed. A tyrant king was confiscating all boats in the area. By disabling the boat of the generous ferryman, al-Khidr (as) was ensuring that his boat would not be seized. The young boy he killed was destined to be wicked and destroy his believing parents with grief. By dying young, both the boy and his parents were saved. Allah then replaced the son with a pure daughter who would become the mother of prophets. The wall had belonged to a good man who, before he died, had hidden a treasure beneath it for his orphaned sons. By preserving the wall from the ungenerous villagers, al-Khidr (as) was protecting the inheritance of the boys until they were grown. All of these actions had been acts of mercy, regardless of how harsh they appeared. And most importantly, as al-Khidr (as) says, **"I did it not upon my own command."** (18:82). He had acted only on the command of a caring and compassionate Lord.

This should have reminded Musa (as) of his own experience. He had been put at risk in a small, unseaworthy craft and set afloat on the river in order to protect him from a tyrant. He had killed a man who was oppressive to others. He had offered his services to the daughters of Shu'ayb (as) beside the well in Madyan in order to protect them from the threat of the herdsmen and had not even thought of payment or reward. So why did he require this teaching if its lessons were obvious and had already been learned?

This story is presented in the middle of Suratu l-Kahf which is situated exactly in the middle of The Qur'an. It is recommended to be recited every Friday before the Juma' prayer. It is used often as a teaching story by Muslim scholars and Sufi shaykhs. It was even used by Carl Jung to explain the importance of being open to what you cannot immediately understand. Without the appropriate knowledge, the world does not make sense. But how can you acquire knowledge if you do not know the means for acquiring it and do not possess the firmness required for holding on to it or the wisdom for applying it? Scholars say that the story illustrates, by means of Musa's (as) deficiencies, the fundamentals of how to learn: keep company with a man of truth (*suhbah*), listen and observe without questioning or complaining (*adab*), be steadfast and obedient even when you do not understand until it is made clear to you (*sabr*).

Some scholars say that the purpose of this story is to illuminate the differences between levels of knowledge. Musa (as), since he brought the Tawrah, represented the Law, the exoteric teaching. He was given awareness of the value of things in order to judge their merits and keep order. Al-Khidr (as), on the other hand, was given a more subtle kind of inspired knowledge that allowed him to see beyond appearances into the secrets of destiny and divine purpose. Among those holding this view there is debate on which is more lofty, the station of Musa (as) or that of al-Khidr (as). Most, but not all, decided that, although the knowledge of al-Khidr (as) is greater, the station of Musa (as) as prophet and confidant of Allah is more sublime. Allah knows best.

These explanations all entail the belief that somehow, in some way, Musa (as) in this story is an example of failure. The Prophet Muhammad (sas) himself is recorded as saying, "We would have wished that Musa had been patient; then Allah would have narrated more of their story" (Sahih Bukhari). Some say that this hadith indicates that Musa (as) should have behaved differently; that, somehow, he was tested and failed. However, it seems more likely that the Prophet (sas) wished Musa (as) had been more patient in order that *we* could take benefit, not so that Musa (as) could have taken more benefit. Musa (as) was one of the greatest of Allah's messengers. He had undoubtedly learned what it was that Allah wished him to learn. So the question becomes, when and what did he learn? What big change is evident in his story that indicates the presence of a new perspective?

The first command Allah gave to Musa (as) at the site of the burning bush, was to go to Pharaoh (repeated six times in The Qur'an). Only after despairing of Pharaoh's redemption, was he commanded to take charge of the Banu Isra'il and lead them through the sea. On the farther bank, they encountered a new spiritual landscape and a new command. This was particularly clear after their momentum was checked at the Jordan River by a forty-year pause. Musa (as) had marched, banners flying, to victory over Pharaoh. Ahead of him was the promised land and the opportunity to establish God's kingdom on earth. But his people were not behind him. They did not know how to follow, as he had not known how to follow al-Khidr (as). Now he was rather abruptly asked to become a patient teacher of unpromising adults and small children. A sign of this perhaps was that his mighty magical staff no longer produced dragons but instead turned dry rock into a source of water for thirsty families. Perhaps Musa (as) needed to experience what it feels like to attempt to follow a teacher who, by definition, one cannot follow. Just as the average person is not equipped to imitate or follow a prophet whose station is way above their reach and yet they are required by God to try.

Sayyiduna al-Khidr (as) riding the big fish and carrying the small one. India 1860.

When describing His slave, al-Khidr (as), Allah says, **one of Our slaves, unto whom We had given mercy (*rahma*) from Ourself, and whom We had taught knowledge from Our Presence** (18:65). The first gift He mentions is *rahma* and, only secondarily, knowledge. It is the word by which our Lord chooses to call Himself, *Ar-Rahman*, *Ar-Rahim*, the most Compassionate, the most Merciful. **Call on Allah or on *Ar-Rahman* - whatever names you call Him, the best names belong to Him.** (17:110). Derived from the same root as 'womb' it denotes loving kindness, empathy, compassion. Out of His love and compassion, Allah fashioned the whole of creation and only by means of His continuous love does creation continue to exist.

As some shaykhs (Ruzbihan Baqli d. 1209, Abdu l-'Aziz al-Dabbagh d.1719) understood the story, Musa *Kalim-Allah* (as), the one Allah Almighty chose to be His confidant, was so absorbed in his conversation with the Almighty that the affairs of his people seemed a distant murmur, insignificant perhaps or irrelevant. As soon as they had crossed the sea in safety, he ran from them in haste to the sacred mountain. He left the tribes to be a sacrifice to their own desires and shaytan. He gave his brother strikingly obvious and basic instructions, **"Take my place**

among my people, and be upright, and do not follow the way of the mischief-makers." (7:142). In so doing, he was perhaps betraying his own recognition that Harun (as) might not be up to the task. But he left anyway.

The concern of al-Khidr (as), on the other hand, is not to lead a nation but rather to protect and elevate all people in fulfillment of Allah's promise to preserve His religion and the believers. He is minutely aware of the details and circumstances of each individual. As the story shows us, he is given insight into their provision, their hearts, and their destinies. He was even given awareness into aspects of Musa's (as) character that Musa (as) himself did not acknowledge. He knew what Musa (as) could tolerate and what he could not. However, even if Musa (as) had been given knowledge of these things, he had little interest in them. His eyes were on the heavens. He was content to leave Harun (as) and Yusha' (as) to deal with mundane matters on his behalf. Now, however, he was confined to the desert wastes and assigned the task of training and educating a new generation. To raise children, to bring them up in the light of faith, one must be intimately aware of their inner condition. It is necessary to recognize for each individual heart when is the right time to reward or punish, to support or admonish, in order to bring about the desired result - a whole and beneficent self, someone whose hand, whose tongue, whose heart will not cause harm to themselves or others - a Muslim.

Ibn 'Arabi (q) has written that each prophet must look after his nation in the most suitable and best manner. It is in this aspect that some of the Perfect Men excel others. (Chittick 1982). Musa (as) needed to be attuned to the individual human heart in order to administer the proper treatment and bring each member of his flock to their own perfection. It was as if al-Khidr (as) was saying, "O Musa, come back down to earth. Before asking for more knowledge, ask for *rahma*. You have to pay attention to your people, to look at them with the eye of compassion, with the gaze of your Lord's love. You have to see where they are and what they need; if their boat needs to be scuttled until the tyrant within is subdued; if their rebellious inner child needs to be mercifully eliminated to make way for a believer; if their treasure needs to be protected and hidden until their self-oppressor is rendered harmless. If you just give orders, no one will follow you. You must lead with love and understanding. O Musa, **Be rabbani, because you are teaching the Book and studying it** (3:79). Be a loving master to your nation."

Yusha' (as) was not taken along on the journey because there was no need at this time for him to keep them company. He was not yet of their station. He might even have misunderstood and lost heart or lost faith from seeing his beloved master humbled and seemingly at a loss. He would learn whatever he needed from Musa (as) at the appropriate time. His heart was already secure in submission and in love. As the Prophet (sas) was told to say, "**If you love Allah, follow me and Allah will love you and forgive your sins. He is the Forgiving, the Merciful."** (3:31).

If Musa (as) did not excel in exemplifying these qualities, Yusha' (as) did. Allah has placed in the background of this story, in the shadows of the great men, a young boy standing quietly to one side holding an empty basket. He is the perfect exemplar of all those qualities necessary to be an obedient servant of Allah. He has a guide with whom he keeps exclusive company (*suhba*). He never objects to his actions or disobeys his command (*adab*). He patiently waits on the shore for his return (*sabr*). He is himself an empty basket waiting to be filled. Yusha' (as) is the third point of the triangle, the resolution of opposites, the perfect balance - the *fata,* the champion of pure heart and the middle way. It is he who will be handed the banner and lead the people into the Promised Land when the time is ripe.

Maqam in honor of Harun (as), Jordan.

13.
Harun (as) Changing Worlds

Musa (as) and Yusha' (as) returned to their people in the wilderness. For forty years the children of Isra'il (as) lived in a no man's land, fed by their Lord, taught by His messengers. The old ones passed away having been protected from any more opportunities to defy their Creator. The young ones grew up strong and pure, accustomed to bare landscapes and spare living, under the fatherly care of their prophets. Forty years produced a new generation, a whole new world. The disconnected, straggly collection of self-serving tribes were slowly being transformed into a united, organized, dedicated force of spiritual warriors although they were still far from perfect and retained their familiar traits of skepticism and complaint.

Musa (as) and Harun (as) were also getting elderly, they were both well over one hundred years old. However, neither their strength nor their mental capacity had diminished nor had they lost an iota of their zeal for serving God. In fact, they felt themselves to be so young that they did not prepare for death or think that it might be near. They could only see how much work there was yet to do before Allah's will was established on earth. Yusha' (as), in the prime of life, had yet to marry or establish a family. His dedication to his Lord and to His prophet left him no time or desire for anything else.

One day Allah Almighty ordered Musa (as) to take his brother Harun (as) on a journey up a mountain overlooking the valley where the people were encamped. The sides of the mountain were steep, nearly vertical, and Harun (as), for the first time in his life, felt fatigue and became out of breath. Rounding a corner, they were surprised to see a house and a garden. In the garden was a bed of rugs spread out beneath big trees whose thick leafy canopy made a deep and inviting shade. Harun (as) asked Musa (as) if he could rest there for a while before they continued their journey. Musa (as) saw what his brother did not, Azra'il (as), the angel of death, sitting quietly with his wings folded around him leaning his back against one of the trees. Musa (as) suggested sympathetically that Harun (as) take a nap on the soft rugs out of the heat of the sun.

Harun (as) was shy to sleep in someone's garden without asking permission but there appeared to be no one home and he was so tired. The whole place had a magical attraction, peaceful and good. Harun (as), longing to lie down there in the cool shade, insisted that Musa (as) lie down with him. He had always trusted his younger brother's judgment and he would not take an action without his lead. He knew that if Musa (as) did something then it must be lawful because Musa (as) was the law personified. If not, then when the owner returned, he would at least find them both guilty of trespass. The two elderly prophets lay down side by side on the piled rugs and Harun (as) drifted into a thankful sleep.

Azra'il (as), the angel of death, unfolded his many luminous wings and approached the brothers. Musa (as) lay quietly with his eyes only half shut, waiting for what he knew was coming. Gently, with compassion and care, Azra'il (as) beckoned to the soul of Harun (as) to separate itself from the body in which it had dwelled for so long. Harun (as) awoke and looked at Musa (as) with reproach. Why had he not protected him or at least warned him? Why had he led him knowingly to this place and this meeting? But Musa (as), obedient to his Lord in all things, reminded him that there was no escaping death. Harun (as), trusting the true words of his beloved brother, released his soul willingly and went with joy to the meeting with his Lord.

Musa (as) read the funeral ritual over his brother's body and prayed for his blessed soul. He remembered their time together and mourned the loss of his companion of over a century, whose support in all situations and kindness in every circumstance had helped to lighten the weightiness of their mission. Then he looked about for some place to dig a grave but before he could, the angels returned and took Harun (as) with them up to the heavens.

Musa (as) addressed his Lord with worry. Without a body or a grave, he feared his people would not believe his story. They would accuse him as usual of some despicably impossible thing. But Allah told him to return to the children of Ya'qub (as) and let them mourn their prophet. Musa (as) descended the hill and entered the camp alone. The people looked, they questioned, they consulted each other, and they began to whisper. Finally, they accused Musa (as) of having done away with his brother out of jealousy because, they said, they had loved Harun (as) more. Harun (as) had been gentle while Musa (as) was fierce. Harun (as) had nurtured them for long years in Egypt while Musa (as) had been nowhere around. Harun (as) had led them through the fearsome sea while Musa (as) had goaded them like cattle from behind. Harun (as) had not punished them for their excesses and their sins while Musa (as) had cursed them to their Lord. Harun (as) had spoken softly and kindly while Musa (as) had given them commandment after commandment. Musa (as) could only look at them in sad resignation and say, **"My people, why do you hurt me when you know that I am sent to you by God?"** (61:5).

Musa (as) took a delegation of people back up the mountain but when they arrived at the spot where the house, the garden, and the wonderful trees had stood, there was no longer any trace of them. This only increased the Banu Isra'il in evil thoughts and accusations. Then Allah in His mercy sent the angels back down with the body of Harun (as) still lying on the bed so that the doubting people could see. Allah returned breath and life to Harun (as) for just enough time for him to sit up on his bier and exhort the people to respect his brother Musa (as) and believe him and follow him in all things. Then he lay back down and breathed his last. For the final time in this life, Harun (as) defended and supported his brother as he had been entrusted to do by his Lord so very long ago. Only then did the people finally accept the truth of what Musa (as) had told them.

They made a memorial tomb for Harun (as) at the very peak of the mountain where it still stands today. Visible from faraway in every direction, it looks out over the barren rolling hills of Jordan still far to the south of the Promised Land.

Then Musa (as) resumed the task of educating and guiding his people without rancor or anger. He had presumably gotten used to their readiness to believe the worst. But the Prophet Muhammad (as) did reflect once in sympathy, when even the Muslims accused him of not being fair, how many unjust accusations Musa (as) had had to endure.

Maqam and small church in honor of Harun (as), St. Catherine, Sinai.

Maqam in honor of Musa (as) near Jerusalem.

14.

Musa (as) Changing Worlds

Two years came and went. Musa (as) was one hundred and twenty years old. Forty years had elapsed since the Banu Isra'il had refused to follow their prophets into the land Allah had given them because of their fear of the giant people who occupied it. Musa (as) had seen all his cohorts, his old companions, buried in the sand and even his beloved brother had been taken in death. Remaining were only two men who had been born in Egypt, Kilab (ra) and Yusha' (as). But still he did not consider death an option. He could not imagine a life of peace or rest. His whole life had been a struggle in the name of Allah and he had no reason to wish it to end.

One day Azra'il (as) came to pay him a visit. Musa (as) saw him coming and was not welcoming. In fact, Musa (as) raised his fist and struck the mighty archangel squarely in the face knocking out one of his eyes. The Angel of Death, whose steely heart and iron hand had not flinched at ripping a child from its mother's arms or a lover from his beloved, flew stunned and crying to his Lord. Allah righted his eye and consoled him. Never again did Azra'il (as) dare to openly approach a living human being. Thereafter, he hid himself from sight so as to never encounter the anger of mankind again. And Musa (as) considered that he had eliminated the threat, at least for the time being.

Allah loved his prophet and did not want to cause him pain or distress. He promised not to take his soul without his consent. There is a Hadith Qudsi that tells us that Allah has said, "I do not hesitate about anything as much as I hesitate about [seizing] the soul of My faithful servant: he hates death and I hate hurting him" (Sahih Bukhari). But Allah also wanted His servant to long for death, however disagreeable, because it leads to the meeting with Him. By one account Allah gave prophethood to Yusha' (as) and began speaking to him in revelation separately from Musa (as). When Musa (as) would ask Yusha' (as) what their Lord was telling him, Yusha' (as) had to respond honestly. He asked his teacher if ever he had asked him about his private conversations with Allah. Musa (as) had to admit that, no, Yusha' (as) had never done that. And so, saddened, Musa (as) stopped asking and, it is said, began to long for death.

It is also said that one day Allah sent Jibra'il (as) to Musa (as) telling him to spread his large hand on the back of a cow. However many hairs his hand covered, Allah agreed to give him that many additional years of life. Musa (as) asked, "And then what?" "And then death" was the reply. **Every soul will taste death. Then to Us you will be returned** (29:57). There was no other way to reach his Lord and he would not be made an exception. So Musa (as) accepted the beauty of his own death.

One day Musa (as) was invited to meet with his Lord at the top of a tall mountain near where the Banu Isra'il were encamped. He picked up his staff and said farewell to his wife, sons and grandchildren. He went last to see Yusha' (as) to tell him he was leaving. Yusha' (as) sensed something unusual and, after a little hesitation, he ran after him and just managed to catch hold of the hem of his coat. Musa (as) shrugged the coat off smoothly and moved swiftly on, leaving his loving disciple standing with his master's mantle grasped tightly in his grieving grip.

At the top, Musa (as) was shown the Promised Land stretching out before him, lush and fertile, a beautiful scene. Then his Lord showed him something of the events that would befall his people in the years to come, both the righteous and the wicked, the kings but also the tyrants, the victories and the terrible defeats. It was a hard road ahead and Musa (as) for the first time felt tired. He had already traveled such a long distance at the head of his people and suffered their infidelities and their deceit. He was weary. There by the side of the path he saw two men digging a grave. It looked deep and cool down in the moist earth and when the men asked him if he would lie in it to see if they had made it long enough, he consented willingly. Once stretched out in the grave, the men revealed themselves as angels and he realized that he had made his choice. His Lord had tricked him but it was fair and fitting. It is said that Allah Almighty took the soul of His friend, Musa *Kalim Allah* (as), with a kiss. At the top of the mountain, with a view of the Holy Land on which he had never set foot, Musa (as) died and was buried by the angels. Not one human eye was there to witness.

It is said by the People of the Book that his grave lies somewhere at the top of Mount Nebo in Jordan but no one knows for sure. If he was not buried there, then that could be where he spent his last hours. Several thousand years later, the Prophet Muhammad (sas) revealed that Musa (as), before he died, had asked his Lord to make his grave as close as possible to the Holy Land, just within sight of it. The Prophet (sas) said he could see the grave site "by the side of the road behind the red sand hill." Many years later another mighty warrior for Allah, Salahuddin al-Ayyubi, saw in a dream the location of that hill and built a mosque and maqam for Musa (as) only ten kilometers outside of the holy city of Jerusalem.

Yusha' (as) went out in search of his master but could not find him. Allah revealed that He had taken Musa (as) to Himself and that Yusha' (as) had inherited the robe of prophethood. It was his duty now to succeed his master in reciting the Book and in leading the children of Isra'il by its teachings into the Promised Land. When Yusha' (as) announced this to the people they were dubious. Most had expected the sons of Musa (as) to be his successors or those of Harun (as). Yusha' (as) was too quiet perhaps or too young, more of a follower than a leader. It was rumored among the people that Yusha' (as) had killed Musa (as) for his own gain. That night Allah sent to all the tribal leaders the same dream in which an angel testified firmly to the innocence of Yusha' (as). When asked in the dream how he had found the most gentle of deaths, however, Musa (as) replied that it had felt as if he were a sheep being skinned alive.

And so Yusha' (as) was raised to fill the station of his beloved master as his most worthy inheritor. This must not have been for him an easy transition. He was too humble to imagine he was up to the task, too respectful to ever assume his master's place, too devastated at the enormity of the loss. The Bible gives us an idea of just how hard it was for him. Allah had to support Yusha' (as) with words of encouragement, telling him not to fear but to follow in the steps of his master Musa (as) without looking left or right. Certainly, this battle-tested hero was not lacking the necessary bravery, but to take on the sacred trust, to don the mantle of prophethood, to slip out of the shadow and into the light - this was daunting even for such a man. And it took Allah telling him three times to "Be strong and courageous," and assuring him, "As I was with Moses, so I will be with you; I will never leave you nor forsake you" (Joshua 1:5-8) before he resolved to shoulder the trust of completing Musa's (as) mission.

Similarly, who can imagine the state of Sayyiduna 'Ali (kw) who lost his Master (sas), the man who had been to him as a father, a brother, a prophet and then, only a few months later, his beloved wife Fatima (rah), his dearest consolation, the mother of his young children, the last remaining physical presence of the Prophet's (sas) luminous immediate family?

About Yusha' (as) it says in the Bible, "He who tends the fig tree shall eat of its fruit and he who waits on his master shall be honored." (Proverbs 27:18).

Musa (as) in his grave with the Banu Isra'il accusing Yusha'(as). Jami' al-Tawarikh by Rashid ud-din, 1305.

Balaam and his Donkey. Rembrandt 1626.

15.
From the Highest to the Lowest

It is not possible to say whether Musa (as) did his job well or not, because apparently the basic nature of a people does not change. The Banu Isra'il continued to be obstinate, argumentative, and suspicious, a nation very difficult to command. But perhaps this is just what Allah Almighty liked about them and why He chose them. They were not easy to teach but what they learned they clung to with persistence. The new generation, however, raised by the prophets in the wilderness, was neither cowardly nor weak. They were more than ready to pick up where their fathers had failed, and to fight valiantly behind their prophet.

Yusha' (as), himself, though of a humble and studious nature, had developed by demand into a wise leader and heroic warrior. Allah's description of the companions of the Prophet Muhammad (sas), **hard against the disbelievers and merciful among themselves** (48:29), is also a good description of him. Given more and more authority by Musa (as), he had taken charge of training the youth to fight and defend themselves. He had organized them into an orderly and fearless army. To give them experience he led them on forays along the borders of the rich green land of Canaan that had been promised them by their Lord but which they had not yet been given permission to enter. Now as the forty years were coming to an end, he led them against small city states on the eastern and southern borders of the Promised Land. Their successes increased the fear of the people already living there. Their neighbors in the settled, well-watered lands to the north began to have concerns about the threat that was poised on their southern borders.

The native people are referred to collectively as Canaanites although at the time they were divided into a multitude of city states each taking its name from the king who ruled them. Each city had its own army and protected itself against its neighbors with thick stone walls and fortifications. Some of them were allied in confederacies and some were not. The Qur'an calls them *jabbarin*, which can mean both tyrants and giants. Some say they were actually physically taller and stronger than other people although archaeologists have yet to find physical evidence to support this. Some say they are simply called giants in order to impress upon us the miraculous successes of God's chosen people in achieving victory over them. Some others say, as was discussed earlier, that these giants were descendants of the dissolute children of Adam (as), a race of people who follow their appetites and have no sense of justice or mercy; children of Qabil (Cain) and his sister Anaq. The *Jabbarin* of Canaan were too proud to acknowledge the authority of their Creator or of His messengers. Allah warns, **Do not strut arrogantly about the earth: you cannot break it open, nor match the mountains in height.** (17:37).

One of the small city states, Balqa, had a plan for a way to deal with the impending threat on their borders. They had among them a prophet of their own, or perhaps he was only a soothsayer or a diviner. This man had come to recognize Allah as the one Lord even while the rest of his people continued to worship a multitude of idols. It is said he had been given knowledge of the hundredth and secret name of Allah Almighty; the name by which, when Allah is addressed, He responds and when petitioned, He grants. This man was named Bal'am ibn Ba'ura (Balaam the son of Beor). He was not a giant himself but he lived among them. Some say that he was actually born of the Banu Isra'il, a companion of Qarun in Egypt. The desire to be the prophet of his own community had driven him to leave the company of Musa (as) and Harun (as). But most contend that he was a native Canaanite, a man of their religion, who had by Allah's mercy been rightly guided and rewarded with the power to pray for the salvation of his people and to predict the future.

Rather than being a giant, Bal'am is described as a sort of dwarf, without friends or family. Because of his lack of height, the daughters of the giants could or would have nothing to do with him. He lived in poverty and depravity with his donkey as his wife. Some go so far as to give him the attributes of the Dajjal, lame in one leg and blind in one eye. Perhaps this is the best way to understand him. Like the Dajjal, who in the last days will be given the power to enact miracles and deceive people into thinking he is God, so Bal'am, for reasons known only to Allah, was endowed with real spiritual authority which he misused. Even though he was not a giant in stature, his disobedience was gigantic and his knowledge only increased him in darkness. The Qur'an exhorts us to **Relate the story of the man to whom We sent Our signs, but he turned away from them: so satan followed him up, and he went astray. (7:175).**

The king of Balqa came to him begging that he pray against Musa (as), that he curse him with the hundredth name. At first Bal'am spoke truly to the king "Woe to you! This is a prophet of God and with him are the angels and the believers. How can I pray against them? I will lose both this world and the world to come" (al-Tha'labi). The king promised him wealth and women beyond count. Bal'am, though tempted, still resisted. Finally, the king threatened grisly punishment and death. At this Bal'am finally relented and agreed to do what was asked of him. He formulated a curse against Musa (as). Some say Allah did not grant it. Others say that Allah did grant it and it was the reason that Musa (as) was denied entrance to the Promised Land. When Musa (as) heard of this, he in turn asked that Bal'am's knowledge of the sacred name be stripped from him so that he could cause no more harm. Musa's (as) prayer also was answered and Bal'am watched in dismay as the holy name exited his heart in the form of a white dove. **Allah has the most beautiful names. So call upon Him by them, and keep away from those who abuse His names. They will be punished for what they used to do. (7:180).**

Still the Canaanite giants believed that Bal'am could save them. It is said that one of the powers that Bal'am still retained, was to know which attribute Allah was manifesting at any given moment. His plan was to wait until Allah was in a state of divine wrath and then make his curse. But Allah knew His servant's plan and He refrained from anger. So Bal'am waited for no purpose. By the time he decided to proceed, Musa (as) had already left this world and been received into the next. Allah had designated Yusha' (as) as His prophet and inheritor and the Banu Isra'il had surprisingly mobilized behind him, for once in agreement and unity.

Bal'am mounted his little donkey who, laboring under his bulk, and resentful of the way she was treated, began to climb slowly to the top of the hills from where they could look down on the encampment of the Banu Isra'il. Every few meters the donkey would stop and refuse to move, as donkeys are wont to do. But Bal'am became exasperated and began to beat her mercilessly. She complained to her Creator and Allah in His compassion gave her human speech. She said "O Bal'am, don't you see the angels who are blocking our way? Are you really going to curse a prophet and the believers?" Then Bal'am squinted his crooked eye and noticed the angels. He fell to his knees to ask forgiveness. But shaytan, the deceiver, whispered to him cunningly and convinced him, as he had Pharaoh, that Allah had actually sent the angels to open the way for him. Bal'am, eager to believe the lie, proceeded up the mountain. Neither the little donkey nor the majestic angels bothered any longer to try to save him from himself. As for shaytan, he will say on Judgment Day: **"I had no power over you except to call you, and you responded to my call, so do not blame me, blame yourselves." (14:22).**

Finally achieving the heights, Bal'am looked down over the Lord's chosen people. He opened his mouth full of foulness and curses but all that exited were blessings. He had promised long before to only utter the words that Allah put in his mouth and so that is just what happened. His heart spoke curses but his mouth pronounced blessing. The king was infuriated and threatened him with death. Bal'am tried again and again. He contorted his lips, he spat, he slobbered, he sputtered. His tongue grew long until it hung thick and heavy in the dirt at his feet. But the words generated by his twisted heart flowed out of his mouth as the loveliest of blessings; blessings on the house of Ya'qub (as) so fine that the Jews, somewhat surprisingly, continue till today to repeat them in their morning rituals.

Allah had shown great favor to Bal'am, choosing him as one of the very few non-Isra'ilite prophets. And yet he threw it away for nothing. There is no created being high enough to be secure from falling, not even a prophet, not even Azazil who became Iblis. **If it had been Our will, We should have elevated him with Our signs; but he inclined to the earth, and followed his own vain desires. His similitude is that of a dog: if you attack him, he lolls out his tongue, or if you leave him alone, he (still) lolls out his tongue. That is the similitude of those who reject Our signs; So relate the story; perchance they may reflect.** (7:176).

Bal'am decided, since he had already lost the hereafter, he would try to get the best of this life using his wit to save the enemies of God. He could have counseled them to make peace with the believers and to accept the prophets as their masters. But rather than submit, he used guile and deceit to lead his people in opposition. He suggested to the Canaanites that they dress up their daughters in diaphanous gowns and send them into the camp of the Banu Isra'il ostensibly to sell fruits and vegetables. The Canaanite girls were exceptionally lovely and Bal'am knew the young men would have a hard time ignoring them, even though it was not permitted to the children of Ya'qub to marry other than girls of their own people. They would commit sin, Allah would punish them, and the unbelievers would be saved. It was a clever, demonic plan and it played out just as Bal'am envisioned.

The girls sashayed into the camp of the Isra'ilite army and took it by storm. One commander in particular, by the name of Zimri, was seduced by the beauty of Cozbi, the daughter of the Canaanite king. He went to declare his intentions to Yusha' (as) who severely reprimanded him and advised him not to disrespect the Lord's prohibition. But Zimri was deaf to his warning. His hand in her hand, he announced publicly that he was taking her regardless of what his prophet or his Lord decreed. Then he carried her into his tent. No one stepped forward to stop him and, in consequence, many others followed his lead.

It was a short time after the death of Musa (as). Yusha' (as) was perhaps still unsure of the degree to which his people would support him. They were poised on the border of the Holy Land, set to engage the enemy in battle. Yusha' (as) was presented with the same sort of dilemma faced by Sayyiduna 'Ali (kw) at the beginning of his term as *khalifa*. To make the analogy even more striking, the Shi'a claim that Saffura (rah), the widow of Musa (as) encouraged a rebellion against Yusha' (as) for the inheritance rights of her sons. But this accusation is counter to both Jewish and Sunni Muslim histories which attribute to Saffura (rah) no whisper of opposition. To enact capital punishment on one of his tribal chiefs, to pursue miscreants within his own ranks was a decision Yusha' (as) was not at that time apparently willing to make. He withheld his hand and waited for a sign from Allah.

The sign came quickly. The next day Allah sent the plague. People sickened and died until seventy thousand had been placed in their graves. Then Fin'has (Phineas) (ra) the grandson of Harun (as), whose position as high priest was by inheritance and firmly established, seized his iron lance and strode to the tent of Zimri. Entering inside, he speared the sinning couple with one thrust. Raising them high over his head, skewered together on the shaft of his lance, he marched around the Isra'ilite camp shouting, "Ya Allah! This is how we treat those who disobey You." Allah accepted his justice as prescribed by the Law and lifted the plague. Yusha' (as) marshalled what was left of the Banu Isra'il and together they marched on Balqa and wiped it and its gigantic people off the face of the earth.

Bal'am was left to the judgment of his Lord. He began to bray like a donkey and munch on hay. No one could bear to be near him. Not even the beasts could understand his grunts and growls. He was handed over to Yusha' (as) for justice but when Yusha' (as) saw the state of Bal'am, he began to shed tears and turned his face away. He would neither punish him nor put an end to his misery. What became of him no one knows for sure although some say he was killed in one of the battles that ensued. There is a grave site at Egerli Dag near Erzurum in Eastern Turkey that is said to be Bal'am's. It lies by itself alone on a hill. Those who approach have said that it reeks of hot tar, particularly potent in summer, and that the earth covering it is boiling. Who visits there once, never visits again. (Evliya Çelebi).

Some say that Bal'am could not have been a prophet because Allah does not give such gifts to those who are unworthy or to those who are unable to hold on to them firmly (Ar-Razi 12th century). But Allah teaches His creation by means of every possible example. **Surely, We created man of the best stature then We reduced him to the lowest of the low** (95:4-5). Bal'am served as an example of how man's stature can shrink because of the state of his heart. He became a spiritual dwarf, reduced by cowardice and depravity from the highest to the lowest. **How foul is the image of those who reject Our signs! They wrong themselves: whomever Allah guides is truly guided, and whomever Allah allows to stray is a loser. And We have certainly created for Hell many of the jinn and mankind. They have hearts with which they do not understand, they have eyes with which they do not see, and they have ears with which they do not hear. They are like animals or even more astray. It is they who are the heedless.** (7:177-179).

Yusha' (as) said, "O Sun, you are a servant of Allah and I also am His servant, give us a few more hours of your light." (Sahih Muslim).

16.

The Commander of the Sun

Yusha' (as) was the first and the last ruler the Banu Isra'il accepted wholeheartedly until the coming of the prophet-king Dawud (as) four hundred years later. Where he led, his young dedicated army followed. They marched against the outlying city states and, one after another, they conquered and put to flight whoever opposed them. They began to eat hungrily from the orchards and food depots of the vanquished enemy. One day the Banu Isra'il woke to find no *manna* covering the ground and no *salwa* waiting to be plucked and eaten. This was a sign for them, which they hardly noticed, that the forty years of blessed punishment had come to an end.

It was now time to reach out and take what Allah Almighty had promised Ibrahim (as) and his descendants - that is Canaan, the Holy Land across the Jordan River. For Muslims, the Holy Land is called Ash-Sham. It includes Damascus and everything within a 3 days camel ride. But Canaan, to the Muslims, consists primarily of Jerusalem, called Al-Quds, the Holy. What makes it holy is that in its center, is the rock of Ibrahim (as) where the Prophet Muhammad (as) led all the previous prophets in prayer and from which he stepped out of this world into the heavens and the presence of Allah Almighty. This is the second place designated holy by the Lord of the worlds at the time of creation. This is the third holiest spot on this earth after Mecca and Medina. In the view of the Muslims there could be no goal of the prophet Yusha' (as) other than to repossess and re-consecrate this sacred place.

The Banu Isra'il had not been able to stay in one spot long enough during their wandering to circumcise those born after leaving Egypt. In consequence, the first thing Allah Almighty ordered Yusha (as) to do was to prepare sharp flint knives for the circumcision of the nation. They camped on the eastern side of the Jordan River and purified themselves and rededicated themselves to serve their Lord. After they had healed, Yusha' (as) led them to the banks of the river. It was spring and they found it in full flood, the rushing current permitting no crossing. They stopped and made camp again, confused and dispirited.

They had not been present when their fathers followed Musa (as) out of Egypt to the edge of the wild sea. They had not seen the roiling waves pull back on either side to form the walls of a liquid passageway. They had not felt the dry floor of the sea firm beneath their bare feet. But Yusha' (as) had been there. He had run his fingers across the walls of water and stared into the round eyes of the startled fish. He knew what his Lord could do. Lifting his hands in prayer he petitioned Allah to open the river for him as He had opened the sea for Musa (as) and Harun (as). Allah heard the prayer of His prophet and once again He parted the water to make a dry path for His chosen to cross to the other side.

Yusha' (as) had also been a witness when the dried fish leapt into the water and sped away through a tunnel Allah had created within the current. He knew this was a spiritual journey on which they were about to embark. It was more than just a river the believers were asking to cross. The priests led the way with the wagon holding the *Tabut*. When it reached the middle of the river safely, Yusha' (as) commanded them to stop. Turning his back to the Ark and the open path, he faced his soldiers. According to a hadith of the Prophet (sas), Yusha' (as) said, "Do not come with me if you have just taken a wife and you are longing for her arms. Do not come with me if you have pregnant sheep and camels and are anxiously awaiting the births. Do not come with me if you have just raised the walls of a house and have yet to affix the roof." In other words, "If your minds and hearts are occupied with worldly concerns, do not come with me. I want only those who are whole hearted and single minded, who are ready to leave everything behind in service to Allah." He said this because he was a prophet looking for sincerity of heart, not for numbers of swords. (Sahih Muslim).

It is interesting that the name for the confluence of rivers that make up the wide Jordan valley is called the *shari'a* in Arabic. From this word the Muslims took the word for the Law of Islam, the straight, wide, and open road. Yusha' (as) the inheritor of Musa (as), the inheritor of the Tawrah, which literally means the Law in Hebrew, could access the citadel of the Holy Land only by means of the *Shari'a*.

Yusha' (as) led the way as he always did, a commander at the head of his troops, the first into danger. The hearts of his men, unlike those of their fathers many years before, soared in courage and determination, thrilled to the proof of their Lord, ready to follow Yusha' (as) wherever he might lead. Ahead of them lay the fortress city, home of the giants. The Tawrah says it was the city of Jericho (Ariha) but the Muslims do not all agree on this. For them there was only Jerusalem (Iliya as it was known at the time of the Prophet (sas) or Quds). It was the only worthy prize and the whole country is subsumed under the name of its sacred city. For six months (six days according to the Tawrah) Yusha' (as) and his men camped under the high walls unable to break them, unable to breach them. Yusha' (as) counseled patience, their Lord would deliver on His promise if they were steadfast. They waited, eager for battle and the chance to prove themselves. But still the walls did not open as the sea had done and they found no way against the giants.

Yusha' (as) sent two spies to scout out the city to try to discover some weakness by means of which they might enter. The spies, however, were detected. The city gates were locked and an alarm sounded. Just as they were about to be caught, a woman signaled to them from the shadow of a doorway of a house built right up against the outer wall. She was a poor woman, who struggled to provide for her parents and siblings. The Bible says her name was Rahab (rah) and she was forced into prostitution in order to care for her family. But the word for prostitute (from the root z-n-h) is also the word for innkeeper so she may have just rented out rooms in her house to others. The Bible, both Old and New Testaments, is very free in ascribing immorality to independent women. Any woman not under the watch of a man was suspect, even the close followers of the prophet 'Isa (as).

Rahab (rah) knew only too well the tyranny of the giants and their lack of mercy, charity, or kindness. She had heard accounts of the Banu Isra'il and of their prophets. Her heart was drawn to them, to their God and to His justice and generosity. She quickly hid the spies on the roof of her house and sent the soldiers running in the opposite direction. Then, under cover of night, she helped the men climb back over the outer wall with ropes she knotted out of her clothes and bedding. In exchange, she asked them for a promise of security for herself and her family if and when they entered the city victorious.

The next day was a Friday, the most blessed day of the week. There is one moment in the course of each and every Friday in which all prayers are answered. That year Friday fell on the tenth of Nissan. We know this day as the tenth of Muharram, one of the most blessed days of the year. Adam (as) was forgiven on that day. The ship of Nuh (as) came to rest on that day. Musa (as) led the Banu Isra'il across the sea on that day. It is a day of mighty events, and new beginnings. Now on this auspicious day, Yusha' (as) the prophet of God, planted himself directly before the gates of the enemy city. His young army stood in restless ranks behind him. In a commanding voice he gave the first *takbir*: "Allahu Akbar! Allah is Greater!" The children of Isra'il (as) joined in: "*Allahu Akbar!* Allah is Greater!" The earth, with a tremendous roar, joined in: "*Allahu Akbar!* Allah is Greater!" A resounding shout, a sharp shake, and the walls of the giant fortress came tumbling down. Yusha' (as) led his troops over the rubble into the heart of the city.

Most of the giants had been crushed under the falling walls. The ones who were left began to fight savagely for their lives. It is said that a whole troop of believers would leap on the back of one giant and still struggle to sever his head. They fought until the sun began to get low in the sky. Yusha' (as) realized that if the battle wasn't won by the time the sun set, they would have to stop fighting. The next day was the Sabbath, the day the Lord had ordered them to leave all worldly concerns and devote themselves to worshiping Him. If they didn't achieve victory by sundown, the giants would escape and the day would be lost. Yusha' (as) put his faith in Allah. Climbing to a high place above the chaos of battle, he faced the setting sun and addressed it directly. "O Sun, you are a servant of Allah and I also am His servant, give us a few more hours of your light." (Sahih Muslim).

The sun listened to the request of Yusha' (as) as the sea had listened to Musa (as). The Prophet Muhammad (sas) said, "The sun was never detained for any human, except for Yusha' during those days in which he marched towards the Holy House (of Jerusalem)." (Musnad ibn Hanbal). However, there is another hadith (as-Suyuti) stating that once, when the Prophet (sas) was traveling with Sayyiduna 'Ali (kw), revelation came upon him as it sometimes did in a very heavy fashion. The Prophet (sas) lay wrapped in his cloak with his head on 'Ali's (kw) knee. Sayyiduna 'Ali (kw) dared not move a muscle until the revelation was completed. When the Prophet (sas) sat up, he saw the sun setting and asked 'Ali (kw) if he had prayed the afternoon (*'Asr*) prayer. When 'Ali (kw) said that he had not, the Prophet (sas) asked Allah to order the sun to climb back in the sky that they might perform the prayer in its time. This event likely occurred sometime after the Prophet (sas) had made the first statement. The course of the sun was changed for both the *fata* of Musa (as) and the *fata* of Muhammad (sas).

The Banu Isra'il continued to fight for however long it took to eliminate whatever giants had not been killed in the earthquake. All living things were slaughtered that day: the giant tyrants, their women and children, and even their animals, by the order of Allah Almighty. No trace of the race of Cain was to be left on the face of the earth. Only Rahab (rah) and her family were saved. After the last giant had met his end, only then did the sun set in a blaze of red.

Allah says, **Fighting is ordained for you, though you dislike it. You may dislike something although it is good for you, or like something although it is bad for you: Allah knows and you do not.** (2:216). However, He also says, but **peace is best** (4:128). There is a time and a place for everything. It was the destiny of both Yusha' (as) and Sayyiduna 'Ali (kw) to spend most of their lives on the field of battle. Although they disliked it, it was due to their dislike that they did it properly. They meted out God's justice with firmness where it was prescribed and with mercy where it was permitted. They did not oppose either their own destiny or that of others.

There is archaeological evidence that Jericho was a large city with two or three thousand inhabitants at around the time of Yusha' (as). Built on a hill, it was surrounded by orchards and fields of grain, watered by the nearby Jordan River. It had a high outer wall of stones and mud brick over fourteen meters above ground level and an inner wall and tower of the same. These were found shattered as if by earthquake and fallen to the outside providing what amounted to a ramp for invaders to climb up into the city. Only one area of the outermost wall is left standing and there, a small house was found leaning against the ramparts, certainly the poorest and least protected area of the city. This perhaps is the house for which Allah promised His protection because it belonged to His servant Rahab (rah). Inside the city there is evidence of widespread fire and ash as if the whole city was burned after the walls fell. The granaries contain huge clay jars scorched by fire but some still untouched and full of winter wheat after the spring harvest.

A section of the northern wall of Jericho which did not fall, where the house of Rahab (rah) most likely stood.

An elderly Yusha' (as) discovers the thief of a piece of cloth from the spoils of war. Jami' al-Tawarikh by Rashid ud-din, 1305.

17.
The Lure of a Grain of Wheat

After they had vanquished the enemy, Allah said to them, **"Enter this town (*qarya*) and eat freely there as you will, but enter its gate humbly (*sujjadan*) and say, '*hitta*'. Then We shall forgive you your sins and increase the rewards of those who do good."** (2:58). But the wrongdoers substituted a different word for the one they had been given. So, because they persistently disobeyed, We sent a plague (*rijz*) down from the heavens upon the wrongdoers. (2:59).

When they were told, 'Enter this town (*qarya*) and eat freely there as you will, but say, "Relieve us!" (*hitta*) and enter its gate humbly (*sujjadan*): then We shall forgive you your sins, and increase the reward of those who do good,' (7:161) the wrongdoers among them substituted another saying for that which had been given them, so We sent them a punishment (*rijz*) from heaven for their wrongdoing. (7:162)

There are four words in these two sets of verses that are interpreted slightly differently by the masters of scriptural interpretation, *tafsir*. The first is *qarya* translated above as town. Some say it means Ariha (Jericho), some say Al-Quds (Jerusalem), and some prefer a broader definition that includes all the conquered areas that Allah was giving to the Banu Isra'il as their homeland. The noun *qaryah* is derived from the root *q-r-y* meaning to collect or gather. It can refer to any place where people are gathered together, big or small, city or state. In this case, according to most of the commentators, it is referring to Jerusalem in particular as that was the place of greatest value and significance even though at the time of Yusha' (as), it is thought that there was no major city there and no battle that took place. The Tawrah, on the other hand, associates Joshua (as) mainly with the conquest of Jericho.

Babu l-Hitta, Jerusalem

The next word is *sujjadan*, meaning prostrate or in *sajda*. It is the first command in *ayah* 2:58 and the second command in *ayah* 7:161. Some narrators say that what was meant was for the Banu Isra'il to crawl on their faces into the ruined city. Some claim that the gate through which they were commanded to enter faced the *qibla* and so they bowed down as in prayer. There was said to be a gate to the holy sanctuary, the *Baytu l-Maqdis*, that was so low that anyone entering by it was forced to bow low to the ground or crawl on their knees. It is claimed that this was the gate by which they were meant to enter. The Prophet (sas) explained in a hadith that the Banu Isra'il, instead of crawling forwards with their faces to the ground, entered the gate backwards on their bottoms with their noses held high in the air in a posture of arrogance. The common understanding is that they were commanded by Allah to be humble in their victory for **It was not you who killed them but Allah who killed them** (8:17). Instead, they entered the area as exultant conquerors. In a story about vanquishing giants, the victors are told to make themselves small so as not to claim greatness.

The third word is ***hitta***. Lane derives this word from a root meaning to unburden or seek relief. Interestingly the common word for sin in Hebrew is *heta*. Specifically, it bears the meaning of a sin done unintentionally, straying from the straight way by mistake, an error. The combination results in the common understanding of this word as being, "Ask to be relieved of the burden of your errors." So, the followers of Yusha' (as) were told that after the amazing victory of their meagre forces over the fortified giants, they were to remember Allah and be humble and thankful. But they did not do this. Instead, the Prophet (sas) said they changed the word *hitta* to the word *hinta,* which means a grain of wheat in Arabic. Given permission to take over the cities and their farmlands in humbleness and gratefulness, instead many of them acted with pride and greed. They entered the city essentially like hungry jackals, howling, "Bread, bread" in anticipation of the vast vats of winter wheat.

Some jars still full of wheat discovered in the ruins of Jericho.

Allah wanted the Banu Isra'il to testify in both word and deed. Their bodies should have been in an attitude of submission, *sajda*, and their tongues in an awareness of humility and gratitude. Essentially, they should have entered the Promised Land, the Holy Land, in a state of prayer. However, similar to their ancestors, Adam (as) and Hawwa (rah), who ate from the forbidden tree in Paradise, mankind once more disobeyed his Lord on account of the lure of a grain of wheat.

The last word needing explanation is *rijz* above translated as plague in the first case and punishment in the second. The scholars agree that it means punishment of which plague is considered one variety. Because of this, some believe that plague was sent to the Banu Isra'il at this point rather than after the affair of Cozbi and Zimri. Some believe that a plague was sent for a second time. Allah knows best.

The Banu Isra'il gathered up all the wealth and property belonging to their enemy and, under the command of Yusha' (as), they built an altar and set all the spoils on it, dedicated to Allah Almighty. Then they waited. Since the time of Adam (as) this was the how the believers made sacrifice in the name of Allah. If Allah accepted the sacrifice, He sent a fire from heaven to immolate the offering. But this time no fire descended. It was revealed to Yusha' (as) that someone among his soldiers had kept something from the unclean spoils of war. He ordered that all the men file past him taking his hand and rededicating themselves to his service. One man's hand stuck to his and he recognized this as a sign that this was the guilty one. The man had hidden a golden ornament in the shape of the head of a cow or, according to others, a piece of velvet cloth. Yusha' (as) ordered him to place it among the other spoils on the altar. As he did so, a flame descended from above and consumed the offerings, the stolen goods, and the thief himself.

The children of Ya'qub (as) took thirty of the city states of Canaan on both sides of the Jordan River, expelling the giants or exterminating them. Before declaring war, Yusha' (as), gave them the choice of becoming believers in Allah or of making a treaty of peace and becoming the vassals of the believers. If they refused both choices then, if they were conquered, they were killed. The Tawrah says that men, women, children, young, old, everyone who opposed them was punished with death and anything that belonged to them was burned as sacrifice.

The Prophet Muhammad (sas) offered his enemies the same choices but he was not ordered to kill the survivors. They were held for ransom or kept as slaves. The Muslims, however, were permitted to take the women in marriage and foster the children. The spoils of war were also forbidden to the Muslims until after the battle of Badr when the Muslims took some of the enemy captive and held them for ransom. Then Allah allowed His warriors to take the weapons, wealth, and riding animals of the enemy to enhance their own meagre supplies rather than to depend on ransom.

The conquest of Canaan was complete. The warriors of Allah were fierce and they were victorious. By the decree of Allah, they showed no mercy to those who themselves had been tyrannical and unmerciful. The Prophet (sas) tells us that "Who is not merciful to others, Allah is not merciful to him." (Sahih Muslim). The Book of Joshua, the sixth book of the Bible, however, tells us something a little different about the manner of the conquest. In it Allah says, "I sent the hornet ahead of you, which drove them out before you... You did not do it with your own sword and bow. So I gave you a land on which you did not toil and cities you did not build; and you live in them and eat from vineyards and olive groves that you did not plant." (Joshua 24:12-13). The Jews and the Christians have no explanation for these verses other than to suppose that at that time there lived in Canaan enormous hornets whose sting was lethal. They posit that the giants ran from these insects and left all their property and wealth behind. Modern scholars give support to similar theories and say that, contrary to all the verses that explicitly say the Banu Isra'il took Canaan by force, they simply moved peacefully into empty cities. The hornet, or some pestilence called by the same word, or earthquakes, expelled the unbelievers but did not bother the believers. Perhaps the nomadic Banu Isra'il, having no need of stone houses or cities, were unaffected by earthquakes.

The vocabulary of Islam can perhaps give us another understanding. The word for 'hornet' in Hebrew means something that stings. In this instance, the word is a singular definite noun - *the* hornet, not the indefinite plural, hornets. In Arabic, the Archangel Jibra'il (as) is called, *an-Namus al-Kabir* which means the large mosquito, the big stinging one, according to Lane's Lexicon. The Jews in fact considered Sayyiduna Jibra'il (as) an enemy (2:141) because he delivers the punishment of Allah as well as His revelation. In particular he causes earthquakes. In light of this, we could understand these verses to mean that Allah sent His Archangel ahead of the army of believers, as He sent him with angelic troops to help the Muslims at the time of the Prophet (sas). Jibra'il (as) put fear in the hearts of Allah's enemies and routed them even before the human soldiers had raised a sword. **It was not you who killed them but it was Allah who killed them** (8:17). *La hawla wa la quwwata illa bi Llah.* There is no power or strength except with Allah.

And every willful tyrant fails (14:15).

Above is a picture of the remains of an altar found on Mt. Ebal near Nablus. It has been dated to the time of Yusha' (as). Below is a sketch of what it must have looked like intact, which conforms to the specifications detailed in the Tawrah.

18.

The Portion of the Sun

After less than seven years, the enemy was vanquished and the land opened for settlement. Yusha' (as) was given the formidable task of apportioning it among the tribes to everyone's satisfaction. This was no minor feat. Even the Prophet Muhammad (sas) faced criticism from his people resulting from his division of the spoils of war. But with God's guidance, Yusha' (as) managed the almost impossible. He had no interest in wealth or position for himself. His only interest was being just in the eyes of Allah according to His Book. He knew the Tawrah from the inside out and could interpret and apply its orders with deep understanding. He was like Sayyiduna 'Ali (kw) whose justice and subtlety in applying the law were well recognized by all the rightly guided *Khalifas* who were known to consult him in difficult legal matters. The Prophet (sas) had told them, "The hand of 'Ali and my hand are equal in justice." (al-Tabari, Nisaburi, Tirmidhi).) Both Yusha' (as) and 'Ali (kw) were nursed from childhood on the Holy Books and grew to manhood nourished by the wisdom of prophets. They saw with the Book, heard with the Book and thought with the Book. And they could read its signs in the world around them. And Yusha' (as), just like Sayyiduna 'Ali (kw), judged by the Book with *rahma* (mercy).

There were twelve tribes of the Banu Isra'il, each descended from one of the twelve sons of the prophet Ya'qub (as). Each tribe received its own territory except for the tribe of Levi which was the tribe of Musa (as) and Harun (as). The descendants of the sons of Harun (as) were chosen by Allah to be the priests, while the other Levites became teachers, temple attendants, or temple guards. A portion of every sacrifice was theirs and the people supported them with gifts. They lived in the vicinity of the places of worship and they governed the cities that grew up around them as sanctuaries. Like the Haram Sharif, anyone who entered was safe. The tribe of Levi did not live off the land and so was apportioned no land.

The tribe of Yusuf (as) was divided into two, descendants of his two sons, Ephraim and Manasseh. Accordingly, the division was still into twelve parts just as Allah divided the year into twelve months. It is said that twelve is a sacred number because Allah chose it for keeping time. **The number of months in the sight of Allah is twelve - so ordained by Him the day He created the heavens and the earth** (9:36). Twelve came to mean completion. Twelve of anything was a complete set, a dozen, a sign of heavenly order. There are twelve bright stars in the northern hemisphere and twelve visible stars in the southern hemisphere all of which were known in antiquity (Schimmel). The sun and moon pass through twelve houses or stations. There were twelve disciples of 'Isa (as). There were twelve men of Medina who pledged themselves to the Prophet (sas) at 'Aqaba. Even though there might not have been exactly twelve actual tribes participating in the apportionment, it is thought that the number was maintained to keep it complete.

The tribe of Judah, the eldest son, received the territory directly around Jerusalem which was not yet a fortified city or even the religious center. Yusha' (as) chose for his own tribe, that of Ephraim, a landlocked territory in the hills north of the center of Jerusalem. In particular he asked for himself a place called Timnath-Heres. This name means "portion of

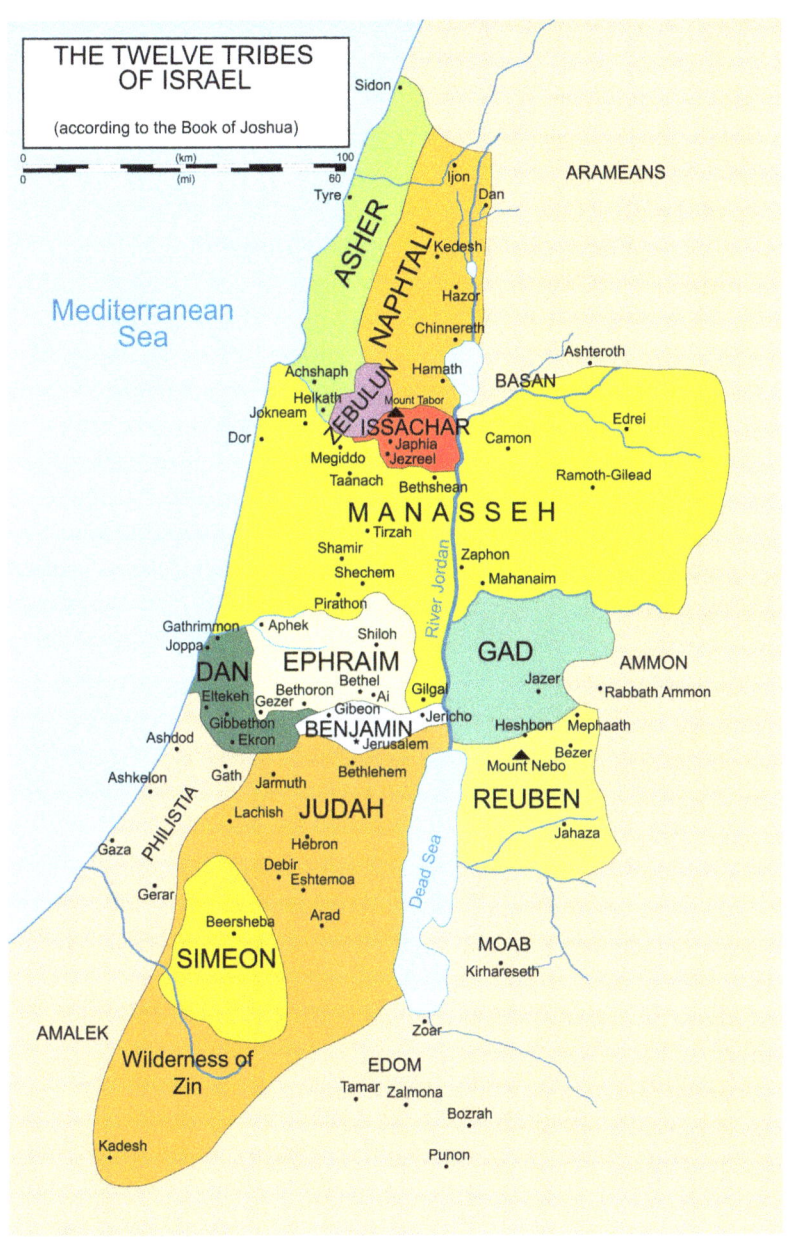

the sun" and it was Yusha's (as) portion, the land of the one who could command the sun. The territory of Ephraim included Bethel (Bayt Allah) the place near which Ibrahim (as) first settled and set up an altar to the One God; the place where Ya'qub (as) later experienced his night journey (*'isra*) from which he got his name Isra'il and later had his dream of ascent to the heavens (*mi'raj*). It was a place so sacred that the priest Fin'has (ra), the grandson of Harun (as), placed the *Tabut* first at Bethel before moving it a little farther north to Shiloh still on the edge of the territory of Ephraim. It was at Shiloh, in the presence of the *Tabut* that Yusha' (as) formally distributed the Promised Land among the people to whom it had been promised. And it is said that he ordered the settlers to plant the bulb sea-squill (*Drimia maritima*) in straight lines along the borders. Its tall stalks of small white flowers formed something like a natural picket fence and can still be found.

Sea-squill plants.

There remained two other important tasks with which Musa (as) had entrusted Yusha' (as). Before the prophet Yusuf (as) died, he had prophesied that his people would eventually return to Canaan. When they did, he asked that they take his remains with them and rebury him in the land of his ancestors. This had also been the request of his father Ya'qub (as). Yusuf (as) had personally escorted the body of his father back to be interred in the cave of Machpelah next to his grandfather Ishaq (as) and great-grandfather Ibrahim (as) in what is now known as Khalil or Hebron. Musa (as) managed to miraculously locate the body of Yusuf (as) where it had been hidden under the waters of the Nile and the Banu Isra'il had carted his remains with them across the sea and for the full forty years in the desert. Since Musa (as) never entered Canaan himself, he left Yusuf's (as) bequest to be fulfilled by Yusha' (as).

Once peace had been established, Yusha' (as) buried his great-grandfather in the Holy Land as he had requested. The Book of Joshua says he buried him near Shechem. Many believe that Yusuf (as) is buried beneath a small *qubba* shrine outside the city of Nablus, which is the site of the ancient Shechem. This tomb has been the site of much recent conflict between the Muslims and Jews. However, many of the early Muslim historians have said that Yusha' (as) laid his great-grandfather Yusuf (as) to rest in or near the cave in Hebron next to his ancestral fathers and mothers: Ya'qub (as) and Layka (rah), Ishaq (as) and Rifqa (rah), and Ibrahim (as) and Sara (rah). This does seem to be the most appropriate and blessed location but Allah knows best.

The other important duty that Musa (as) had entrusted to Yusha' (as) was that, when he had secured the Holy Land, he should build a large sacrificial altar at the foot of one of the mountains bordering Shechem (Deut. 27:4-7). An altar at that time meant a large raised stone platform on top of which offerings were slowly immolated. It had many specifications detailed in the Tawrah as to its size and shape. It must be built of "unhewn stones", have a ramp instead of stairs, a grill to allow ashes to fall below and places for the blood to drain. Such a structure has been found by archaeologists on the slopes of Mt. Ebal on the north side of the city of Nablus (Shechem). It fits the description and seems to be dated to the approximate time period. It is possible that it could actually be the remains of the altar built by Yusha' (as).

Shiloh was the sacred capital of the Banu Israil at the time of Yusha' (as) because it is where the *Tabut* rested, holding a **remnant of that which the house of Moses and the house of Aaron left behind**, (2:248). All of the land was considered sacred but most sacred was the place where the *Tabut* encamped. It was the place from which Allah spoke to His people, the residence of the *Sakina*. It remained a moveable sanctuary for four hundred years until the prophet Dawud (as) built it a permanent stone home on the Temple Mount in his chosen city. It was at Shiloh in the presence of the *Tabut*, that Yusha' (as) released his soldiers from duty, divided the land, and sent them off to settle into their new homes.

Yusha' (as) had no desire and no permission to take on political authority. After his work as military commander was done, after he had established the supremacy of Allah's Word in the land, he left governing to the tribal elders. The people, without hesitation or sign of regret, took leave of the man who had served them, and guided them, and led them to a physical and spiritual victory. They headed off excitedly to take possession of their own pieces of earth; wanderers dependent solely on Allah no longer but proprietors with homes and gardens and business to attend to.

There is a hadith of Sayyiduna 'Ali (kw) which attributes to Yusha' (as) the name Dhu l-Kifl. He was asked who are the prophets having more than one name. He replied, "Yusha' (as) who was known as Dhu l-Kifl; Ya'qub (as) who was known as Isra'il; Al-Khidr (as) who was also known as Baliya ibn Malikan (al-Tabari and al-Kisai) or as Abu l-Abbas; Yunus (as) who is called Dhu n-Nun; 'Isa (as) who is called al-Masih, and Muhammad (sas) who is known as Ahmad." (Muqaddasi). Others have said the title refers to Ezekiel (as) (usually called Hizqil in Arabic), or perhaps Ayyub (Job (as)). The word *kifl* means to fold, particularly to fold in half so Dhu l-Kifl means possessor or master of the folding, dividing. Some have said that this prophet wore a cloak of double thickness (A.Yusuf Ali) or that he parted his hair in the middle (Amina Adil). Muhammad Asad translates it as "one who has pledged himself to God" because the word *kafala* can also mean to be a guarantor or to take responsibility for someone or something.

Yusha' (as) is deserving of this epithet for three reasons: he took on the responsibility for fulfilling the mission of Musa (as), he divided, folded, the Holy Land among the believers, and he was a champion of the middle way. If this is the case then it can be said that he is mentioned twice by name in The Qur'an. **And remember Isma'il, Idris, and Dhu l-Kifl: they were all among the steadfast (*sabirin*) and We admitted them into Our mercy. They were among the righteous (*salihin*) (21:85-6).** And a second time, **And remember Our servants Isma'il, Al-Yasa', and Dhu l-Kifl, all of them among the truly good (*akhyar*) (38:48).**

The tomb of Yusuf (as) on the outskirts of Nablus (Shechem), West Bank.

The opening line of Suratu l-Qalam. **Nun. By the Pen and that which they write!** (68:1)

19.
Some of the Secrets of Nun

In The Qur'an it is said that there are two kinds of guidance: one that is clear and unambiguous called *muhkamāt* and one that is symbolic - parables open to interpretation called *mutashabihat*. (3:7). The one speaks directly to the logical mind and requires attention and obedience. The other speaks to the heart. **We will show them Our signs on the horizons and within themselves until it becomes clear to them that it is the truth.** (41:53). These symbols or stories can serve us as openings into the world of the unseen, the *ghayb*, that in which we have pledged ourselves to believe even if we are unable to verify it with our eyes.

It might be that the patronym, ibn Nun, tells us more about Yusha' (as) himself than it does about his parentage. Ibn Nun might be considered as an epithet, an honorary title like Dhu n-Nun or Dhu l-Kifl. It calls attention to important aspects of Yusha's (as) mission and station that we might otherwise overlook.

Nun is the fourteenth letter in both the Arabic and Hebrew alphabets, expressing the sound 'n'. Its shape in Arabic is that of a cup with one dot inside, to modern eyes much like a bowl with a single fish. In Hebrew it is in the form of a vertical line bent at top and bottom. Both shapes are reminiscent of an Egyptian hieroglyphic from which they both probably derive. In both languages the word *nun* itself literally means fish.

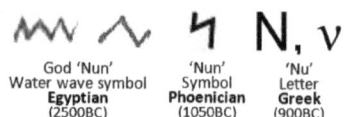

| God 'Nun' Water wave symbol **Egyptian** (2500BC) | 'Nun' Symbol **Phoenician** (1050BC) | 'Nu' Letter **Greek** (900BC) |

Nun. By the pen and that which they write (68:1). There is something very special about *nun* as evidenced by the fact that Allah Almighty swears an oath by it in the first line of the sixty-eighth chapter of The Qur'an, *Suratu l-Qalam*. It is thought by Ibn Abbas (ra) to allude specifically to the angelic fish created by Allah to stabilize and carry the seven earths smoothly through the cosmic sea (al-Tha'labi). On this fish the seven earths rest. His tail and his head curve upward on account of the weight of the burden on his back. He is considered to be related to both of Allah's servants - the fish that swallowed Yunus (as) and took him on a journey through the veils of darkness, as well as the small luncheon fish that returned to life and swam miraculously upstream, witnessed by Yusha' (as) as the sign of the meeting of the seas.

Ibn Abbas (ra) also suggests that the shape of the *nun* resembles an inkwell. **Say: Though the sea became ink for the Words of my Lord, verily the sea would be used up before the Words of my Lord were exhausted, even though We brought the like thereof to help.** (18:109). Or another possibility is that the *nun* might stand for the last letter in Allah's name *Ar-Rahman*, the Most Merciful. Mercy is the ink with which our Creator continuously writes the world. Whatever attribute of Allah's mystery is ascribed to the sea, the fish represents that small part that is accessible to mankind.

As discussed earlier in Chapter 2, one of the oldest meanings that we know for Nun is as a god within the ancient Egyptian pantheon of gods.

Allah created an angel to carry the 7 earths, who stands on a blue-green stone, which balances on the back of a bull, which rests on the fin of a fish, which swims in the celestial ocean, which rides on the wind, which depends on the *Qudrat* (power) of its Lord.

He was, in fact, the source of the gods, the original Creator. He was considered the god of the primordial darkness and the primeval sea. He was the god before the creation of the worlds and all the other gods. His all-inclusive darkness held within its density, everything. For there are two very different kinds of darkness: the darkness that entraps the light and the darkness of the divine mystery out of which all light is born. Out of the dense and sacred darkness, the light emerged and the first thing Nun materialized was the sun god, Ra. This is similar in understanding to the Bible passage: "In the beginning Elohim (Allah) created the heaven and the earth. And the earth was without form, and void; and darkness was upon the face of the deep. And the Spirit (*ruh*) of Elohim moved upon the face of the waters. And Elohim (Allah) said, 'Let there be light: and there was light." (Genesis 1:1-4). **Allah is the light (*nur*), of the heavens and the earth.** (24:35) and from this light He created the light of Muhammad (sas) and from that light, all of creation.

There is, however, an understanding of letters, a science which is said to have been a specialty of Sayyiduna 'Ali ibn Abi Talib (kw) and was explored further by Ibn 'Arabi (q), who wrote that "the *nun* is an immense secret which is the door of generosity and compassion." (Gilis). In this wisdom tradition the letters are experienced as being, not just marks made with a pen, but evidences of the Creator, vocalized breaths and visible lights, living angelic beings. There is more to the letter *nun* than meets the eye. Ibn 'Arabi (q) went further to describe the letter *nun* as being the visible lower half of a circle whose upper half is hidden. The complete form is that of a circle with a dot in the center. This sign has been, since ancient times, a symbol of the sun with the orbiting planets. The apparent and the hidden *nun* unite to become the solar orb, the source of light, *nur*, the symbol of the divine source.

This symbol has also come to represent the hierarchy of saints. The Prophet (sas) said there are kinds of saints because of whom Allah sends the rain and renews the world (Ibn Hanbal). Among them are the forty called the Substitutes (*Abdal*), among these are the four called the Supports (*Awtad*), among these is the one called the *Qutb* (the Pole). These saintly positions have their eternal models in certain of the prophets but at all times they have a living representative on earth to keep watch over creation and to provide a worthy recipient for the blessings of the Creator. This spiritual reality is symbolized by the sun in the form of the double *nun*: half of it is in the world, the living saints, and half of it is heavenly and beyond sight of the common view.

The Prophet Muhammad (sas) has left us two hadith in which he mentions the prophet Yusha' (as) by name. One identifies Yusha' (as) as the young servant, who accompanied Musa (as) in his search for al-Khidr (as) and who was appointed guardian of his sign, the fish. The other hadith is, "The sun was never held back for any human except Yusha', on the days he marched to Jerusalem." (Ibn Hanbal). The fish and the sun are two clues to the secrets of Yusha' (as) and the letter *nun*.

Two of the prophets, who stand as examples of the saintly stations, have a clear solar connection. The prophet Idris (Enoch) (as) was said to be a friend of the angel of the sun and, while on a visit, died there and was resurrected. He remains in bodily existence in heavenly realms. Ibn 'Arabi (q) ascribes to Idris (as) the heavenly role of *Qutb*, the master of the saints. Ilyas (Elijah) (as) is another, whose disappearance from this world on a horse or chariot of fire serves as a symbol of his solar connection.

'Isa (as) and al-Khidr (as), the remaining two of the four heavenly *Awtad*, are associated with the symbol of the fish as a sign of eternal life and heavenly knowledge. Al-Khidr (as) is often represented riding on a fish in much the same way as the angel who supports the world. Yusha' (as), who historically predates all of them except Idris (as), is clearly a member of this honored assembly.

It is interesting to note that in Imam al-Jazuli's (q) inspired poem of praises on the Prophet (sas), *Dala'ilu l-Khayrat*, when he gives salaams on the previous prophets, he does not place Yusha' (as) historically with Musa (as), Harun (as), and Shu'ayb (as) but rather in the group of mystical prophets associated with the protecting hierarchy and the end of time. He places Yusha' (as) in the company of Ilyas (as), between Dhu l-Khifl (as) and 'Isa (as) in the Friday portion and in the same company but next to al-Khidr (as) in the Saturday portion.

After the cessation of prophethood, these saintly functions were taken up by men and women who, by their love for their Creator and care for His creation, have been elevated to fill these posts. In this way it was possible for 'Ali (kw) to say "I am he who in the Injil (Gospel) is called Ilyas (as)" (*Khutbatu l-Bayan*) and also to say "al-Khidr (as) is my brother." Even Pharaoh, the enemy, the perversion of goodness, the inversion of the prophets, was Rameses, son of the sun, to indicate how high his promise and how profound his fall.

Yusha' ibn Nun (as) functioned as the *Qutb* of his time, not just as the center of the sacred hierarchy but as the central point to which all else is gathered and as the access to the means of ascent. He is the prototype of the savior, the messiah. He represents the one who guides the promised into the land promised them, the bearer of the light of Muhammad (sas) enlightening the way of approach to Allah Almighty. **It is Allah who created seven heavens and of earths the same. His command ('*amr*) descends between them. (65:12).** It is said that the Command ('*amr*) of Allah lies between the letter *kaf* and the letter *nun*. With these letters, by means of the word they form, Allah Almighty spoke the creation into existence. He said, **"Kun" fa yakuun, "Be" and it became.** (16:40). Everything comes from Allah and returns to Him. Everything is created complete, with both its beginning and its ending. *Kaf* represents the beginning of the journey, the breathing out, and *nun* represents the journey's end, *nihaya*, the breathing in. Ibn Nun, might therefore be understood as signifying 'son of the return', the savior, the one who leads into the Holy Land which can only be, in truth, the return to God.

All the Peoples of the Book have recognized something of this association. The Jewish tradition mentions the coming of an inheritor from the tribe of Ephraim, son of Yusuf (as), called 'the war messiah', *Meshiach ben Yosef*. Someone like Yusha' (as), he will vanquish the enemies of God at the end of time. The Christians make an association between the first Yusha' (as) and the second who is Jesus the Messiah (as). Some Muslims (both Ottoman and pre-Safavid Shi'a according to al-Ayyashi (d. 932)) predict that Yusha' (as) himself will return physically to serve the Mahdi (as) as one of his generals. According to al-Tabari, when Ibn Abbas (ra) was asked about what happened to the youth (*fata*) who accompanied Musa (as) to find al-Khidr (as), he replied, "He drank of the water of life and was sent in a boat to rock on the sea until the end of time." This serves as an indication that he continues to have a role to play in the unfolding of the destiny of the world.

What is the Holy Land other than the center point of the *nun*, the qibla to which everything turns. The Prophet (sas) described it as being the source of all sweet water, the access to heavenly realms, the gathering place for the Day of Judgement. He defined the saints as the reason Allah sends heavenly rain (*rahma*) (Ibn Abbas). The word *qutb* itself means both a pole of ascension and a place of gathering. Mecca and Jerusalem have each been called the navel of the earth (*surra*), the channel to Allah that sustains and nourishes. They, in turn, spread nourishment to the rest of the world, as Allah Almighty calls Mecca, **umma l-quraa**, the mother town (42:7). The figure of the complete *nun* is a symbol of this reality - of the sun, of the *Qutb*, of the Holy Land, of the light of Allah - the center which by definition can be **neither of the east nor the west** (24:35).

It was the prophet Yusha' (as) to whom Allah Almighty assigned the most sacred task of opening the way to the Holy Land, of connecting the earthly roads with the heavenly highways, and of bringing the believers home. Ibn 'Arabi (q) described the *nun*, however, not as the final goal but as the doorway. Yusha' (as) is the son of the *nun*.

The Ka'ba as the dot inside the inverted Nun and all paths leading to it. 18th century Arabia.

What remains of the large stone set up by Yusha' (as) as a reminder to the believers of their covenant with their Lord. Shechem (Nablus, West Bank).

20.
Farewell

The conquest of the land and its settlement is said to have been accomplished in less than seven years after the passing of Musa (as). Only then, the Talmud tells us, did Yusha' (as) finally marry and establish a home and family of his own. He chose as his home Timnath-Heres on the border of the territory of Ephraim. He chose as his wife, Rahab (rah), the poor innkeeper from Ariha who, guided by Allah, had saved the spies and assisted the Muslims in breaching the walls of her tyrant city. Some say that he and Rahab (rah) were blessed with many children, among them sons, although we have not been told their names or their stories. Others say that they were blessed only with daughters. The Christians, however, believe that Rahab (rah) married someone else and their son became an ancestor of the prophet Dawud (as) and ultimately of 'Isa ibn Maryam (as) (Gospel of Matthew) through his stepfather Josef (ra), a complicated lineage.

The Banu Isra'il were supposedly not allowed to marry foreign women. But it is interesting to note that in spite of this ban, Yusuf (as) married Zulaykha (rah) the Egyptian, Musa (as) married Saffurah (rah) the Madyanite, and Yusha' (as) married Rahab (rah) the Canaanite. Allah knows best.

Unfortunately, the Prophet Muhammad (sas) did not leave us a firsthand physical description of Yusha' (as) even though he must have seen him among the prophets who prayed behind him on the Temple Mount during the Night Journey. And he did not mention Yusha' (as) among the prophets who welcomed him in Paradise. However, the Muslim writers of the stories of the prophets have told us that Yusha' (as) was of medium height and broad shouldered. He had a light brown complexion and large eyes. The Jews have told us that, while he possessed the strength of an ox, he expressed the beauty of a gazelle. He was above all things a humble slave of God. He had grown up in the presence of the greatest of men, Allah's prophets, and he was content to rest in their shadow. He remained silent in their company, listening and watching. He neither bothered them with questions nor drew attention to himself in any way. He waited on them and for them. Whether he accompanied them on journeys or stayed back, whether he was ordered to command an army or to carry their lunch, whether he sat inside the tent or outside the door, whether he studied scripture or waged war – he was always at their service and never in the way.

Yusha' (as) was a study in opposites. In physical prowess and religious zeal, he had the strength of an ox. In personal dealings and spiritual subtleties, he had the lightness of a gazelle. In this way he also resembled what we know of 'Ali ibn Abi Talib (kw), who is described as being medium to short in height, of broad build, with large heavy eyes. He too was both a scholar and a soldier; a humble servant and a fearless leader. He was fierce in war but gentle in peace. He was uncompromising in obedience to the Law but generous in its application. He was hard on himself but tolerant of others. He carried his crushing burdens with apparent ease. And yet never, not for a moment, was he forgetful of the eye of Allah upon him or the eternal consequences of his every breath.

And never, not even for a moment, did his eyes leave their focus on his master (sas).

Yusha' (as) was a charismatic leader whom the Banu Isra'il followed wholeheartedly as their commander and their prophet, something they had been unable to do for Musa (as) or Harun (as). This seems due to divine decree rather than to the personality of Yusha' (as) himself. No one could have been more beloved of his people or more charismatic than the prophet Musa (as) but his people did not know how to follow him. By the time Yusha' (as) inherited them, they had been prepared and trained and were at last ready to put their hands and hearts on the line for their Lord. Or it could have been because, after descending from the mountain, the light of Musa's (as) face was as intense as the sun. He was forced to wear a veil for fear of blinding those who looked at him. Yusha' (as) reflected the same light but in a softer spectrum from which the average gaze had nothing to fear. He was easier to follow.

Whether because of the curse of Bal'am or because he beat the rock too hard to get water, as the Jews claim, Musa (as) was not granted the satisfaction of bringing his mission to completion. For whatever reason, the entry into the Holy Land of Canaan was left to his disciple Yusha' (as). The Prophet Muhammad (sas), on the other hand, was honored with the completion of everything he began. For him, Allah opened the hearts of his enemies and the gates of the Holy Land of Mecca. He attained completion and needed no successor.

Given relief by Allah from the military and political duties of his prophethood, Yusha' (as) enjoyed a few well-earned years of quiet and peace, although he remained available to his people at all times for advice and guidance. He had a small orchard in whose shade he spent his days, wielding a pen, instead of a sword, recording the history of the Banu Isra'il since the passing of Musa (as). In this way also 'Ali ibn Abi Talib (kw) resembled him. There were twenty-five years between the death of the Prophet Muhammad (sas) and the death of the third *khalifa*, Sayyiduna 'Uthman (ra). During this time 'Ali (kw) retired respectfully to his estate at Yanbu. He left everyday governing to those whose job it had become and devoted himself to worship and to compiling and transcribing The Qur'an. He remained available at all times, however, to give advice or assistance in an unofficial capacity whenever it was requested of him.

There are twenty-four chapters that make up what is known today as The Book of Joshua in the Bible. The first twelve describe the conquest of Canaan. The second twelve record in detail the distribution of land and the parting advice Yusha' (as) gave to his people. The book we have now is thought by modern scholars to have been written down during the Babylonian captivity, in 550 BCE or later, almost a thousand years after the events it recounts. However, it may be based on an original text penned by the blessed and careful hand of Yusha' (as) himself. When he wasn't occupied in this way he took to wandering the hills around his home seeking solitude with his Lord and seclusion from men.

For about twenty-seven years, Yusha' (as) served as prophet and leader of his people. He was successful in every way, as military commander and as legislator of the peace. The people loved him and obeyed him and after him no man commanded their obedience and respect for four hundred years until the coming of the prophet Dawud (as). But in his later years he did not have much to do with the organization or affairs of the tribal nations. Each tribal territory was self-governed by its own chiefs. And Yusha' (as) had no desire and no divine command to be king. So he lived quietly in his chosen land. But he became increasingly concerned by what he saw around him. Some say that what disturbed him most was that the Banu Isra'il did not share the knowledge with which their Lord had blessed them. They did not teach or enlighten the inhabitants of the lands they settled. They behaved as if Allah belonged exclusively to them, a tribal God. Yusha' (as) reprimanded them and denounced their arrogance and lack of generosity. But he saw that they did not take his warning to heart.

When he became aware that his time on earth was drawing to a close, he summoned the chiefs of the tribes to gather at Shechem. Then, as was the custom of all prophets, he delivered his last advice and warning, calling Allah to witness that he had delivered the message with which he had been entrusted and that the people had heard and understood.

First Yusha' (as) reminded them of their past. He reminded them how Allah had led their great-grandfather Ibrahim (as) out of Haran and promised him and his descendants the fertile land of Canaan; how Allah had given him Isma'il (as), Ishaq (as) and then Ya'qub (as) and how they had left Canaan to join Yusuf (as) in Egypt. He reminded them how Allah had sent to them Musa (as) and Harun (as) and delivered them from Pharaoh through a miraculous opening in the sea. He reminded them how Allah had fed them and guided them in the wilderness and, finally, how He had delivered the land into their hands, defeating their enemies. Yusha' (as) quietly listed all the many miracles and all the small kindnesses, with which their Lord had favored them. At the end, he presented them with a choice. "Now therefore fear the Lord and serve him in sincerity and in faithfulness … And if it is evil in your eyes to serve the Lord, choose this day whom you will serve … As for me and my house, we shall serve the Lord" (Joshua 24:14-15). And the people replied with one voice. "We will serve the Lord for He is our God." (Joshua 24:18). But Yusha' (as) spoke the truth to them as al-Khidr (as) had spoken to Musa (as): "You are not able to serve the Lord." (Joshua 24:19). However, the people insisted, "The Lord our God we will serve, and His voice we will obey." (Joshua 24:24).

This was written down, as a renewal of their covenant with Allah. And Yusha' (as) set up a stone there in that place as a witness and a reminder of what they had promised. It is believed, since ancient times, that stones in general have the ability to record and remind. Like the stone Tablets of the Tawrah, they can hold within themselves the word of Allah. The *Hajaru l-Aswad*, the Black Stone, is said to be an angel that keeps within itself a record of all people who have visited the House of Allah and greeted it with sincerity. On the Day of Judgment, it will be given a voice to testify.

This was the way of the prophets. In the same way Musa (as) bade farewell to his people and so did Ibrahim (as) and Ya'qub (as). **Were you there to see when death came upon Ya'qub? When he said to his sons, "What will you worship after I am gone?" they replied, "We shall worship your God and the God of your fathers, Ibrahim, Isma'il and Ishaq, one single God: we devote ourselves to Him."** (2:133). In the same way Sayyiduna Muhammad (as) delivered his farewell *khutba* after the completion of his last pilgrimage. He reminded the people to remember that they are accountable to Allah for all their actions. They must be brothers to each other, protect and respect each other. They must hold tightly to what they had witnessed and stay firmly on the straight way by adhering to The Qur'an and his sunnah.

Yusha' (as) passed away among his loved ones and was buried without recorded ceremony or display. He slipped out of this life as he had slipped in, leaving very little in his wake in the way of personal details. He had served his people and his Lord faithfully. He did what was commanded of him without pomp or ceremony, without drama or fanfare. Yusha' (as) passed from this life into the next and was put in the ground in the place that was his, Timnath-Heres, the Portion of the Sun. According to some, he died on the twenty-first of Ramadan, the same day on which Sayyiduna 'Ali ibn Abi Talib (kw) was later martyred (al-Tabari), a date said by many to have been *Laylatu l-Qadr*.

Ibn Kisai says he died at 120 and spent 40 years as a prophet. Al-Tha'labi says he died at 120 and was a prophet for 27 years. Al-Tabari says he died at 126 and that he received prophethood at 99. The Tawrah says he died at 110 and was a prophet 51 years. He lived a long, blessed life entirely devoted to fulfilling the commands of his master the prophet Musa (as) and his Lord. He accompanied and helped guide his nation from slavery in Egypt to sovereignty in Canaan. He, like Sayyiduna 'Ali (kw), was a holy warrior on the battlefields of life, both the inward and the outward.

There is a hadith (Qurtubi d. 1273, al-Wahidi d. 1075) that one day,

Suratu l-Qadr. **The Night of Power is better than one thousand months** (97:3).

when the Prophet Muhammad (sas) was sitting among his companions, he commented on the long lives of the prophets of the Banu Isra'il. Yusha' (as), for instance, had served his Lord for a full eighty years in prayer and spiritual struggle (*jihad*) never failing or tiring. The companions felt sorrow that their own lives would be too short to enable them to worship for an equal number of years. The Prophet (sas) appealed to his Lord who immediately responded by sending Jibra'il (as) with *Suratu l-Qadr*. Allah Almighty gifted the Muslims with one night a year, the Night of Power (*Laylatu l-Qadr*), which **is better than a thousand months** (97:3). The observance of this one night has the value of eighty-three and a third years of prayer and service. Yusha' (as) indirectly provided the occasion for this very special gift from Allah.

In the Old Testament, Allah counseled Yusha' (as) at the time He confirmed him as a prophet, saying "Above all, be strong and very courageous. Be careful to observe all the law that My servant Moses commanded you. Do not turn from it to the right or to the left. The Tawrah must not depart from your mouth; meditate on it day and night, so that you may be careful to do everything written in it. For then you will prosper and succeed in all you do." (Joshua 1:7,8). To these commands Yusha' ibn Nun (as) was true. He succeeded in all he did.

21.
Maqams

As Yusha' (as) predicted, the Banu Isra'il were not able to keep their promise. After the generation that had pledged themselves to worship Allah "had been gathered to their ancestors, another generation grew up who knew neither the Lord nor what He had done for Israel. Then the Israelites did evil in the eyes of the Lord and served the Baals. They forsook the Lord, the God of their ancestors, who had brought them out of Egypt." (Judges 2: 10-12). In order to prevent Yusha' (as) from having to witness the unfaithfulness of his people it is believed that Allah removed him bodily, or at least spiritually, to other more faithful regions.

Where exactly the tomb of Yusha' (as) lies today nobody knows for sure. There are many places throughout the Muslim world that claim to be his resting place. There are at least two possible areas that scholars suggest might be the ancient Timnath-Heres, one frequented and one long deserted. There are other places where he performed heroic deeds to which perhaps his spirit still clings and additional places where great deeds similar to Yusha's (as) own were accomplished with his spiritual assistance. There are again other places where those who love him simply discovered or attracted his spiritual presence. All of these places, *maqams*, are real and true. They are places where his reality can be contacted by the believer because these men of Allah, men of Truth, are not dead. They are ever living and, to the heart that reaches out to them, they reliably respond.

The Tomb of Yusha' (as) Kifl Haris, Nablus West Bank

There is village near the city of Nablus (the ancient Shechem) in the Palestinian West Bank known today as Kifl Haris. It is thought by the Muslims, Jews, and Samaritans to be the ancient site of Timnath-Heres, the home and burial place of Yusha' (as). There is a small domed maqam and prayer place built by the Muslims for Yusha' (as). Nearby are two *mashhad*s, one for his companion Kilab (ra) and another for his father Nun (ra), although many conflate the occupant with the prophet called Dhu n-Nun, Yunus (as). There is also a gravesite nearby for Dhu l-Kifl (as), reflecting perhaps the connection between the names Dhu l-Kifl and Yusha' (as). Allah knows best but it would appear that there is some confusion about the site and about who exactly lies buried there.

The Jewish people commemorate the death of Yusha' (as) on the 26th of Nisan which would correspond to the Muslim month of Muharram except that the Jews have an intercalated lunar calendar enabling Nisan to always occur in the Spring. The tombs were built by Muslims and are said to date from the 10th century rule of Salahuddin al-Ayyubi. There is no evidence that they existed prior to that time although they were rebuilt several times by the Ottomans. Once a year, late at night, on the 26th of Nisan, the police block off all the roads in the village leading to the *maqam*. Jews travel to the village to pray and to read scripture in memory of their prophet. Today, sadly, the village of Kifl Haris has become the site of frequent political debate and violent conflict between the Jews living in a nearby settlement and the Arab Muslim villagers.

The Tomb of Yusha' (as) Khirbet Tibneh, West Bank

There is another site that Christians have identified as the real Timnath-Heres, at a place called Tibneh to the south of Nablus. Set into the northern side of a hill that could be Mount Ga'ash, it fits the Biblical description more closely than Kifl Haris. Unlike that contested and disputed site, Tibneh is currently uninhabited. It is an area of scrub and stones where only the low outline of foundation walls attests to the abandoned presence of an ancient city. Tombs were discovered nearby, cut into the rock in a sort of primitive prototype of the elaborate tombs of Petra. One tomb in particular they believe could have been the place of internment of Yusha' (as). The entryway is large, originally having a row of stone pillars along the front, decorated with a frame of carved rosettes, symbols of the sun. It exhibits evidence of veneration with hundreds of small alcoves cut into the rock face believed by some to be for the purpose of holding votive lights and by others to be niches made much later as nesting places for domestic pigeons. It has a main burial room off the entry with a recess to hold a single body. Then radiating out from this, there are other rooms with spaces to hold family members. It is definitely the tomb of a person whose people continued to honor and remember them.

The Tawrah states that they buried along with Yusha' (as) the flint knives that were used to circumcise the tribes before their victorious entry into the Promised Land. The graves are no longer sealed and have been open to predators and vandals for hundreds of years now but scattered among the debris inside the burial chambers are hundreds of hand-chipped stone blades. The bones and bodies of those interred are gone. Allah would not permit the remains of the ones He loves to be desecrated. Perhaps their absence explains why there are so many alternative places where the physical remains of Yusha' (as) are said to have been divinely resettled. Allah alone knows.

The Tomb of Yusha' (as) As-Salt, Jordan

There is another grave site for Yusha' (as) not too far away on the other side of the Jordan River, near the city of As-Salt This is the site of the Biblical Balqa, where Musa (as) and Yusha' (as) fought the giants together and killed 'Uj. It is known for sure that Yusha' (as) was actually physically in this place because its historical identity is well verified but there is no written record that he died there. However, there is a classical tradition that the spirits of heroes remain near the sites of their greatest victories. The burial mound is a gigantic ten meters long, a testament to Yusha's (as) greatness and his ascendance over his tyrant foe.

The Tomb of Yusha' (as) Baghdad, Iraq

Next to the grave of the Sufi Master Junayd (d. 910 CE) in Baghdad, there is a maqam for Yusha' (as) built over a thousand years ago during the reign of the Abbasids. The religious officials today are confident that this is his actual grave because they say that there was the sign of the sun engraved on the original outer wall. They say it was Yusha's (as) dying wish to be buried in 'Iraq and so Allah made this possible. The caretaker is happy to tell visitors of the angels who guard the building every night in the form of birds and of the snake who lives inside the catafalque and patrols the neighborhood during the day, guarding the tomb itself at night. Yusha's (as) blessing pervades the neighborhood. It is well known by the people of the city that prayers that are asked in his name at this site, are answered by Allah.

The Jews, however, say it is not the grave of Joshua the prophet but rather of Joshua the High Priest who returned from exile in Babylon (Baghdad) to be the first high priest in the rebuilt temple. Allah knows best.

The Tomb of Yusha' (as) al-Minaya, Lebanon

There is a mosque and a grave for Yusha' (as) in Lebanon outside the city of Tripoli. The grave sits inside a natural cave part way up the side of a mountain. Caves seem to be the traditional burial places of the Banu Isra'il. The graves of Sayyiduna Ibrahim (as) and Sara (rah) in Hebron are also inside a natural cave. The cave in Lebanon is narrow and deep. The burial mound stretches from the open entrance all the way to the back, 13 meters. It is a place that is said to have been revered by the Jews of Beirut during Ottoman times and now by both Christians and Muslims. Some say that when Yusha' (as) was dying he was thirsty. A spring opened inside the cave to provide him with water and it continues to flow today in service to Allah's beloved emissary even when other sources of water in the vicinity have gone dry.

It is also said that not far away lie the remains of the village that refused hospitality to Musa (as) and al-Khidr (as) as described in *Suratu l-Kahf*. Again, it is a common occurrence that heroes return to places where tyrants were vanquished thereby ensuring that evil is replaced by goodness, darkness with light.

The Tomb of Yusha' (as) Isfahan, Iran

Just to the southwest of the city of Isfahan there is a cemetery that is called *Takht-i-Fulad* (the Throne of Steel). Some of the oldest grave markers indicate that it has been a cemetery for over a thousand years. But there are many who contend that it has been a place of burial for at least seventy-five hundred years. Over a thousand prophets, many of them from the Banu Isra'il are buried there, in addition to thousands of kings, saints, and scholars along with their faithful followers. One of the oldest parts of this extensive cemetery is called, *Lisanu l-Ard*, the Tongue of the Earth. It is said that Allah Almighty at the time of creation **turned to the heaven when it was smoke, and said unto it and unto the earth: "Come both of you, willing or unwilling." They said: "We come willing."** (41:11). It was from this place that the earth replied in obedience to its Lord and has continued to speak on rare occasions. It was heard to tell people of the presence of the prophet Yusha' (as) buried within its depths. A *maqam* or tomb was built over the spot that is still greatly revered. On the night before Juma', people visit to seek his blessing and intercession with Allah, to heal their sick and to soothe their sorrows. It is a fitting memorial to Yusha' (as), the exemplar of servanthood, to be remembered in the place from which the earth itself expressed its willing submission to its Lord.

The Tomb of Yusha' (as) Beykoz, Turkey

The Ottomans, however, said that once, when he was walking in the Ephraim mountains near his home seeking seclusion with Allah Almighty, Yusha' (as) came upon a stranger. Yusha' (as) greeted the man and persuaded him to sit for a while and tell his story. The man said that he came from a far land where the people were peaceful and kind but that the idle curiosity of youth had enticed him to set out to see the world. He had never found, in all his wanderings, another place on earth as pure and as sweet. Now that he was old, he was full of regret. All he wanted was to be able to find his way home. Yusha' (as) asked about his homeland. The stranger told him that it was far to the northwest but that it looked very much like the land upon which they were sitting. There were green hills and below them a valley with a river running between two seas. They were looking at the Jordan River connecting the Sea of Tiberius to the Dead

Sea. Yusha' (as) in turn told the man his story. He told him about Allah, the one Almighty God and about His favors and His forgiveness. The heart of the stranger opened to faith and he accepted Islam at the hands of Yusha' (as). Now he finally understood why he had left his homeland so very long ago. His whole life had been a journey whose sole purpose was to bring him to this place at this time. After spending some days together, they reluctantly parted company. The stranger set off for his distant northern home, all his regret gone, satisfied that his life had not been a waste. Yusha' (as) returned to his prayers and to his own home.

Many years later, no one knows when, a shepherd was herding his sheep on a hill looking over the Black Sea in Anatolia. He noticed a mound of earth that his sheep would not cross. When herded in that direction, they split into two and circuited around rather than over it. He showed this to others of his people and they recognized that it must be holy ground, the grave of someone beloved by Allah. Yusha' (as) had not lain under the soil of Canaan for very long before he saw and heard his people betray their promise not to worship other than God. He had seen them fight among themselves and commit every sinful, forbidden act. He had been a witness to the many afflictions and punishments the Lord had sent down upon them. His eternal soul began to long for the peaceful land about which the stranger had told him.

But it could also be said that Yusha' (as) continues to accompany the believers whenever and wherever they struggle against tyrants. He accompanied them in battle, whether against Canaanites or Byzantines. The Byzantines actually called Constantinople the "New Jerusalem". Certainly, in the hadith of the Prophet (sas) it had been promised the Muslims – "Verily, you shall conquer Constantinople. What a wonderful army will that army be, and what a wonderful commander will that conqueror be." (Musnad Ahmad, Nisaburi). This is why it is also said that Yusha' (as) will return to support the Mahdi (as) at the end of days. He will rest only when the true Promised Land has been finally achieved.

By permission of his Lord, his spiritual awareness traveled to Beykoz, where it rests now in peace on a high hill overlooking the Black Sea and the Bosporus, still guarding a spot where two seas meet. Yahya Efendi (q), a milk brother of Sultan Sulayman the Magnificent (1495-1566), and a Sufi master, was informed spiritually that the holy presence he felt so strongly on that hill was that of Yusha' (as). It is interesting to note that Yahya Efendi was considered to have attained in particular the station of 'Ali ibn Abi Talib (kw) and to meet with al-Khidr (as) every Juma'. He asked the Sultan to build a mosque and memorial there. Permission was granted and a small mosque was constructed near the grave mound which lies nearby enclosed by a grill-work fence and planted with trees and flowers. It is an enormous 17 meters long.

There are local accounts that relate that Yusha' (as) came to Beykoz for battle. He fought at the bottom of the hill in a place called Sütlüce and was killed there. His body was cut in two pieces, perhaps another explanation for the epithet Dhul-Kifl. The lower part was buried in Sütlüce and from it a spring of healing water rose out of the earth that is called the Water of life (*Ab-i Hayat*), thus connecting Yusha' (as) with al-Khidr (as) and Alexander Dhu l-Qarnayn (as). Only the upper half of his body was buried on the mountain at Beykoz. At this time an army base restricts access to the lower site but there is still a fountain on the mountain.

In addition, it is related that the grave mound originally faced Jerusalem but, when the Muslim *qibla* was changed to Mecca at the time of the Prophet Muhammad (sas), the grave itself turned to face the Ka'ba.

The Bosporus is guarded on four sides by mountains, each of which is the location of a saint. Yahya Effendi (1494-1570) is in the southwest, Aziz Mahmud Hudayi (1541-1628) in the southeast, Telli Baba (d. 1453) in the northwest and Nabi Yusha' (as) in the northeast. Istanbul is reported to have been constructed on the orders of al-Khidr (as) in a vision to the then Byzantine emperor Justinian (d.565). Al-Khidr (as) has been closely associated with the city ever since and there are many places related to him, including a pillar within the Aya Sofia mosque. Yusha' (as) has come to be recognized as one of the patron saints, one of the spiritual protectors of the Ottoman capital. He and al-Khidr (as) together continue to guard one of the gates between seas, between Europe and Asia, between worlds.

The length of the tombs associated with Yusha' (as) from Baghdad to Beykoz attest to the fact that Yusha' (as), the man known to have battled the tyrannical giant enemies of God, has, in his spiritual reality, become a giant of true greatness himself.

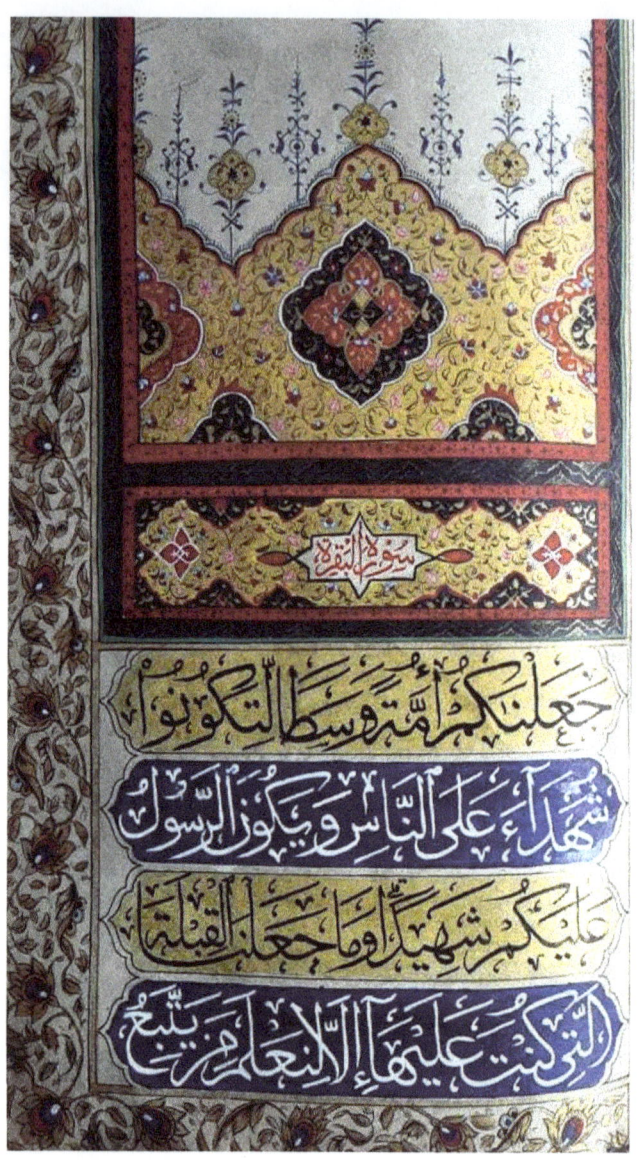

One verse from Suratu l-Baqarah including the phrase, **We made you to be a community of the middle way** (2:143). 16th century India.

Conclusion

The Middle Way

"The mention of Moses has become a chain (obstruction) to the thoughts (of my readers), for (they think) that these are stories which happened long ago. The mention of Moses serves for a mask, but the Light of Moses is thy actual concern, O good man. Moses and Pharaoh are in thy being: thou must seek these two adversaries in thyself. The (process) of generation from Moses is (continuing) till the Resurrection: The Light is not different (though) the lamp has become different." (Rumi, *Mathnawi*, Nicholson trans. 3:1249-1252).

What conclusions can be drawn from a life, any life, but especially from the luminous life of a prophet of God? There are undoubtedly as many conclusions as there are people to draw them. Yusha' (*'alayhi s-salam*) was chosen and his course directed specifically to be a sign, a map for those looking for a way to reach the heavenly pathways. Perhaps there are no conclusions, only lessons to be drawn from isolated glimpses of an interior landscape different from the ones with which we are familiar. For to travel on heavenly roads we need heavenly selves, not these pedestrian selves with which we plod along the alleys of the world weighted down with anger and fear.

Certainly, the most obvious lesson to be derived from the life of Yusha' (*'alayhi s-salam*) is the inverse of the Sufi adage attributed to the Prophet Muhammad (*salla Llahu 'alayhi wa sallam*), "Who has no shaykh, his shaykh is shaytan." Yusha' (*'alayhi s-salam*) was the ultimate follower with the ultimate guide. Since we cannot be our own guides, we need to find someone with whom to practice and perfect the virtues that constitute the middle way, the avoidance of extremes, the way Allah has chosen for us. We need a teacher on the straight way.

The story of Yusha' (*'alayhi s-salam*) might be read as an allegory for the transformation of the self. We are born with a heart and soul that are pure and balanced. This is our God-given, innate nature, our *fitra*. We are in peaceful submission to Allah and in harmony with His creation. As we grow we become corrupted or imbalanced under the influences of our family, environment, and circumstances. Our goal in life must be to restore our selves to their original balance in order to return our soul to our Maker in the same pure state in which we received it.

Allah tells us that the lowest level of the self is the ego, called the *nafsu l-ammarah*, the inciting, tyrant self: **for man's very soul incites him to evil** (12:53). It is prey to its animal desires and, left to take control, it will ruin or obscure everything higher. Its attributes are often characterized as the so-called seven deadly sins: lust, gluttony, greed, sloth, wrath, envy, and pride. Al-Ghazali (*qaddasu Llahu sirrahu*) provides more-or-less, the same list with some additions. He lists its characteristics as: pride; greed and miserliness; backbiting and useless chatter; gluttony; desire for ostentation, power and fame; lust; anger and malice; envy; vanity; and lack of spiritual resolve (*himmah*).

Pharaoh clearly represents the extremes of pride and arrogance. He was swallowed by a sea that opened mercifully for believers. Qarun personifies greed and ostentation, as well as hunger for power. His destiny is to be eternally consumed by the world he so desired. As-Samiri succumbs to spiritual envy and vanity which only resulted in his being banished from all human company. Bal'am is a grotesque and pathetic example of gluttony and animality. He traded the promise of the Hereafter for the allure of the world and was reduced from the highest state to the lowest. Zimri characterizes lust. 'Uj and his kind are the embodiment of anger and malice. The Banu Isra'il themselves display the sorry evidence of lack of spiritual resolve and aspiration. However, they enter into a higher stage – that of the accusing self, the *nafsu l-lawwama*. They begin to recognize their own failings and feel regret. They sin and repent and sin again in a frustrating movement mirrored by the circular wandering in the desert. Harun (*'alayhi s-salam*), Musa (*'alayhi s-salam*), and Yusha' (*'alayhi s-salam*) represent the higher self, the *Rabbani*, godly self, submitted to Allah and serving as His deputies. They might personify the three higher stages of the self (the pleased, the pleasing and the pure).

In this story taken as allegory, the enemies of the higher self are killed or left to die. However, in our inner life, to destroy them is neither useful nor possible. They must, instead, be trained and brought into balance under the control of the higher self. Al-Ghazali (*qaddasu Llahu sirrahu*) says that each ugly attribute is, in fact, either an excess or a deficiency of a beautiful one. An excess of courage becomes recklessness and a lack becomes cowardice. An excess of generosity becomes extravagance and a lack becomes avarice. The cure for any extreme is its opposite. The cure for excess unwarranted pride is to endure shame. The cure for excess talk is silence, for excess eating is fasting, for hoarding is giving, for anger is patience, for rashness is hesitation.

Every virtue is the mean between two extremes. Allah Almighty has informed us that the way He has chosen for us is the middle way. **We made you to be a community of the middle way** (2:143) and the prayer we are told to guard in particular is the middle one (2:238). Middle does not mean simply that it is central but it implies that it is the best, the most excellent. The only people, however, able to truly express the middle way, perfect balance, are the prophets and their inheritors. The Prophet Muhammad (*salla Llahu 'alayhi wa sallam*) embodied its completion. Most of us will achieve a modicum of success by swinging back and forth between the extremes, hitting the middle only occasionally but perhaps reducing the breadth of the swing.

Yusha's (*alayhi s-salam*) surname, *ibn Nun*, also indicates the middle way. The letter *nun* has the numerical value of fifty and occupies the middle of the Arabic alphabet. The fact that Yusha' (*alayhi s-salam*) himself is the third of the three who met at the *sakhra*, at the conjunction, the middle, of the two seas, is another sign. The account of this meeting occurs exactly in the middle of The Qur'an, bridging the fifteenth and sixteenth sections (*juz*) out of thirty. If, as is usually said, Musa (*alayhi s-salam*) represents the divine law and the exoteric and al-Khidr (*alayhi s-salam*) represents the unseen and the esoteric, then Yusha' (*alayhi s-salam*) perhaps is the junction of the two, one foot on each shore. If al-Khidr (*alayhi s-salam*) represents knowledge by means of inspiration, and Musa (*alayhi s-salam*) represents knowledge by means of the Book, then perhaps Yusha' (*alayhi s-salam*) represents knowledge by means of evidence, witnessing. The eye is the organ of sight but it cannot see without light and it cannot interpret its vision without the organ of sensory perception. All three are necessary.

Yusha' (*alayhi s-salam*) is also the third in relation to Musa (*alayhi s-salam*) and Harun (*alayhi s-salam*), perhaps again representing some sort of spiritual middle ground between them. Allah describes His prophet Muhammad (sas) as having three functions, **We sent you as a witness, and a bearer of good news, and a warner.** (48:8). Perhaps these aspects are divided and personified among the earlier prophets. Musa (as) is the warner, Harun (as) the bearer of good news, and Yusha' (as) the witness. The Qur'an also says, **We sent Our messengers with the clear proofs, and We sent down with them the Book and the Balance, that humanity may uphold justice. And We sent down iron, in which is violent force, and benefits for humanity. That Allah may know who supports Him and His messengers, unseen. Allah is Strong and Powerful.** (59:25). In this instance Musa (*alayhi s-salam*) is the Book, Harun (*alayhi s-salam*) is the Balance, and Yusha' (*alayhi s-salam*) is the iron, the warrior who puts justice and mercy into action. This is perhaps why Sayyiduna 'Ali (*karramu Llahu wajhahu*) remembered him by the title Dhu l-Kifl, meaning the possessor of the middle place, champion of the middle way.

What is most remarkable about the story of Yusha' (*'alayhi s-salam*) is that, like the Prophet Muhammad (*salla Llahu 'alayhi wa sallam*) and the prophet Yunus (Jonah *'alayhi s-salam*), he is one of the very few prophets to whom Allah Almighty granted a successful outcome. After much struggle, his nation finally was prepared to follow his lead and submit to Allah's Word. After destroying the enemies within themselves, Yusha' (*'alayhi s-salam*) and his people crossed the river Jordan, called the *Shari'ah* in Arabic. It opened miraculously for them as the sea had opened for Musa (*'alayhi s-salam*). The lower self, tamed and obedient under the guidance of the higher self, called the self at peace (**al-nafsu l-mutma'inna**), then entered through the opening. The soul, conforming to the orders of its Lord, obedient to the *Shari'ah* Law, now found, by means of the Law itself, a way into the Holy Land.

The spiritual warrior, veteran of the ego wars, had, through effort, patience, and humility, gained access by permission of his Lord, to the higher stations of the soul. The noble *fata* entered into what he had been promised: he entered *al-arda l-muqaddasa*, the land that is holy, as close to the Source as he could bear. **But as for you, O soul at peace, return to your Lord well pleased and well pleasing;** (89: 27-28).

The Middle Land

The verse quoted above, in which the community of Muhammad (*salla Llahu 'alayhi wa sallam*) is defined by Allah as belonging to the middle way (2:143), is, perhaps surprisingly, to be found imbedded among the verses that announce the change of *qibla* from Jerusalem to Mecca (2:142-5), from the Farthest Mosque (*al-Masjidi l-Aqsa*) to the Sacred Mosque (*al-Masjidi l-Haram*). This reflects the two main elements of the story, the glory, of Yusha' (*'alayhi s-salam*). He was both the opener of the holy land and the exemplar of the middle way.

Mecca, Medina, and Jerusalem. Decoration for an 18th century Ottoman qibla compass.

A holy land in general is the place where God establishes communication with mankind, a place where the earth connects to the heavens. It is variously described as the navel, the junction, the isthmus. Man, in his complete and balanced form, exemplified by the prophets, is crowned with this same function. He is the vicegerent, the sacred bridge between the creation and the Creator. It is no surprise then to find the holy man connected to the holy place, the man of the middle way opening the middle place, the soul at peace in the land of peace (**daru s-salam**) (6:126-7).

This connection is already hinted at in the meeting that took place at the juncture of the seas where Yusha' (*'alayhi s-salam*) and Musa (*'alayhi s-salam*) found Sayyiduna al-Khidr (*'alayhi s-salam*) the gatekeeper, wrapped in the mantel of inheritance, lying beside the *sakhra* (18:63).

Sakhra means rock but it is specifically used for the sacred rock on the Temple Mount in Jerusalem that was for a brief time the Muslim *qibla* and is still the direction of prayer for the Christians and Jews. That *sakhra* was thought to be the place of sacrifice for Ibrahim (*'alayhi s-salam*), the place where earthly offerings were reduced to smoke and ascended to heaven. That *sakhra* was also the place from which the Prophet Muhammad (*salla Llahu 'alayhi wa sallam*) ascended to the Divine Presence.

The Holy Land is the earthly conduit of heavenly waters and it is described in the image of Paradise: **gardens beneath which rivers flow, wherein they will dwell forever. Allah is pleased with them, and they are pleased with Him.** (58:22). It is a place from which Allah Almighty, **whose throne was upon the water** (11:7), disburses the waters of mercy and eternal life. It has been related by several of the close companions of the Prophet (*salla Llahu 'alayhi wa sallam*) (Ibn Abbas (*radhia Llahu 'an*), Abu Hurayra (*radhia Llahu 'an*), Ubayy ibn Ka'b (*radhia Llahu 'an*) that all sweet water on earth arises from beneath the *sakhra* before being distributed around the globe, even though the Temple Mount in Jerusalem itself has no actual water source except for the Gihon spring that lies at its base. The Ka'ba, however, has the miraculous spring of Zamzam, directly beside it. In addition, the meaning of the name Ka'ba, usually understood as cube, derives from a root whose primary meaning is joint or junction indicating its function as the connecting point of heaven and earth, the center point from which the earthly globe was generated, the welling up of the waters of life.

Abdullah ibn Salam (*radhia Llahu 'an*), a Jewish convert to Islam, once asked the Prophet Muhammad (*salla Llahu 'alayhi wa sallam*) why *al-Masjidi l-Aqsa* (Jerusalem) is called *aqsa*, meaning farthest. The Prophet (*salla Llahu 'alayhi wa sallam*) answered because it is *wasta*, meaning middle. He continued to explain that Jerusalem is middle because it is the location of the Day of Judgment; the place where all the souls will be gathered and it is the base of the *sirat*, the bridge that crosses hell and leads to Paradise (Ibn al-Murajja c. 1020 CE). The Holy Land is the middle because it is the gate between earth and heaven. It is the middle because it sits between death and eternal life. It is called the farthest because it sits at the farthest boundary of earth, closest to heaven. It is the physical locus of the spiritual junction between the two seas.

At the time of Adam (*'alayhi s-salam*), Allah appointed for his benefit and that of his descendants, at least two sacred spots on earth in order to maintain a heavenly connection. First, Allah created the Ka'ba and, after forty years, *al-Masjidi l-Aqsa* (Jerusalem). **The first house established for mankind is the one at Bekka (Mecca); blessed, and guidance for all people** (3:96). These two sanctuaries provide access to His divine presence; places where the perfume of Paradise can still be sensed and where the praises of the angels can still be heard. Both sacred spots were then mostly forgotten and abandoned until the prophet Ibrahim (*'alayhi s-salam*) rebuilt them, establishing one son in each. Forgotten and abandoned once more, Allah sent Yusha' (*'alayhi s-salam*) to reopen and re-consecrate Jerusalem. But Mecca He left veiled in its hidden valley, as He left the seed of Muhammad (*salla Llahu 'alayhi wa sallam*) hidden in the descendants of Isma'il (Ishmael *'alayhi s-salam*).

Mecca remained, however, a site of pilgrimage for all the succeeding prophets. Knowledge of its centrality was concealed but not lost. The Bible testifies: "Blessed are those who live in Your house; They will still be praising You. Blessed is the man whose strength is in You, Whose heart is set on pilgrimage. As they pass through the valley of Baca (Mecca), They make it a spring." (*Zabur*, Psalms 84:4-6).

Towards the end of the sixth century CE, signs began to appear that an important change was beginning to unfold. The walls of the Ka'ba were crumbling and the people of Mecca made the uneasy decision to tear it down and rebuild. Unknown to them, the young man of noble lineage chosen to set the Black Stone back in its corner, was the man who would later be revealed as the Prophet Muhammad (*salla Llahu 'alayhi wa sallam*). Some years later, his uncle's wife, Fatima bint Asad (*radhia Llahu 'anha*), gave birth to Sayyiduna 'Ali (*karramu Llahu wajhahu*), inside the restored sanctuary.

In approximately the year 620 CE the Prophet Muhammad (*salla Llahu 'alayhi wa sallam*) was woken from sleep by Jibra'il (*'alayhi s-salam*) and instructed to pray two *raka'at* at the Ka'ba before mounting the Buraq (*'alayhi s-salam*) and setting off on his journey by night (*Israa*). Three more times he was asked to dismount and  pray - at Medina, at Mount Sinai, and then at Bethlehem - before tethering the Buraq (*'alayhi s-salam*) and leading all the earlier prophets in prayer on the Temple Mount in Jerusalem. From there he ascended to the heavens (*Mi'raj*). It was as if he were threading these holy places on a string of prayer; securing them like beads on a *misbaha* (rosary) to the *alif* of the Divine Presence.

Two years later, in the middle of prayer, the believers were directed by Allah to turn their faces away from Jerusalem to Mecca, the **umma l-quraa** (6:92, 42:7), the mother of towns, the first sanctuary on earth and so, appropriately, the last. As Yusha' (*'alayhi s-salam*) had done for Jerusalem, so Muhammad (*salla Llahu 'alayhi wa sallam*) did for Mecca. He rededicated the Holy House to the exclusive worship of Allah and opened it wide as both the gateway to heavenly roads and the channel of divine mercy. Yusha' (*'alayhi s-salam*), in his *maqam* in Beykoz, immediately turned his face in that direction.

According to al-Tabari, when Ibn Abbas (*radhia Llahu 'an*) was asked about what happened to the youth (*fata*) who accompanied Musa (*'alayhi s-salam*) to find al-Khidr (*'alayhi s-salam*), he replied, "He drank of the water of life and al-Khidr (*'alayhi s-salam*) put him in a boat and sent him to rock on the sea until the end of time." Al-Khidr (*'alayhi s-salam*) himself is said to dwell on an island where the seas conjoin. These are points of spiritual geography which serve as images for the states of people alive on a different plane who are still awaiting the fulfillment of their destinies. The death of Sayyiduna 'Ali (*karramu Llahu wajhahu*) also ended with a question mark. Although wounded in the mosque at Kufa by a poisoned sword, his death was never publicly witnessed. He was interred secretly, it is said, by close family at a place that was much later revealed to be Najaf. However, it is reported that travelers entering Kufa on the day of his death declared that they had greeted him on the road, healthy and strong and riding away in the opposite direction. Both Yusha' (*'alayhi s-salam*) and 'Ali (*karramu Llahu wajhahu*) departed their earthly duties on the twenty-first of Ramadan. It is interesting to note that this was also the date on which the Prophet Muhammad (*salla Llahu 'alayhi wa sallam*) entered Mecca and purified the Ka'ba for the worship of the one God.

The hidden Nun and the open door.

Looking at a map, one can see that these sites are spread pretty much in a corridor running south to north through the Holy Land. Indeed, the line continues north of Jerusalem to Bethel, Shiloh, and Shechem, the spots Ibrahim (*'alayhi s-salam*), and later the *Tabut*, made sacred. Then it continues on to Damascus, whose holiness was attested to by the Prophet (*salla Llahu 'alayhi wa sallam*). It is a channel of sacred space rather than a single point, the fold or the diameter of a symbolic circle, recalling the two *nun*s.

"To Allah belong the East and the West. He guides whom He wills to a straight path." (2:142). Spatially perhaps Jerusalem lies in the center but spiritually it requires entering from the door that is open, and that is in Mecca.

In many ways the story of Yusha' (*'alayhi s-salam*) was a dress rehearsal for the coming of the grandson of Sayyiduna 'Ali (*karramu Llahu wajhahu*), Muhammad al-Mahdi (*'alayhi s-salam*), and the second coming of 'Isa al-Masih (*'alayhi s-salam*). It was another episode in the repeating drama of the human condition: a fall from grace followed by repentance and forgiveness; a temple destroyed followed by its rebuilding; an ejection from Paradise followed by a return.

Yusha' (*'alayhi s-salam*) is the prototype of the messiah, the establisher of absolute justice, the exemplar of the middle way. He, and the men and women like him, occupy the fold between worlds. "By them, the earth is established, and by them you are sent rain, and by them you are granted help and victory." (hadith of the Prophet (*salla Llahu 'alayhi wa sallam*) Tabarani). Putting them in your heart allows them to take you with them into the land that is holy.

The prophet Yusha' (*'alayhi s-salam*), and Sayyiduna 'Ali (*karramu Llahu wajhahu*), continue to invite us, offer to guide us - home. For what else is a holy land if not the home for which we long, the enveloping embrace of the One to whom we belong? It is not the temple walls nor their terrain, not their design nor even what they contain, not the memories of those who stayed there, nor the prayers of the those who prayed there that make it holy. Its holiness resides in the One who made there, in the heart of the believer, His domain.

Allah bless our master Musa (*'alayhi s-salam*) and his *fata*, Yusha' ibn Nun (*'alayhi s-salam*).

Allah bless our master Muhammad (*salla Llahu 'alayhi wa sallam*) and his *fata* 'Ali ibn Abi Talib (*karramu Llahu wajhahu*).

Accept us among their loving followers and their eternal companions in nearness to You. Forgive us and help us to be people of the middle way, *ya Arhamu r-rahimin*.

The journey is to Him, *Jalla JalaluHu*.

If My slaves ask you about Me, I am near. I respond to the call of the one who calls out to Me, so let them respond to Me and believe in Me that they may be guided (2:186).

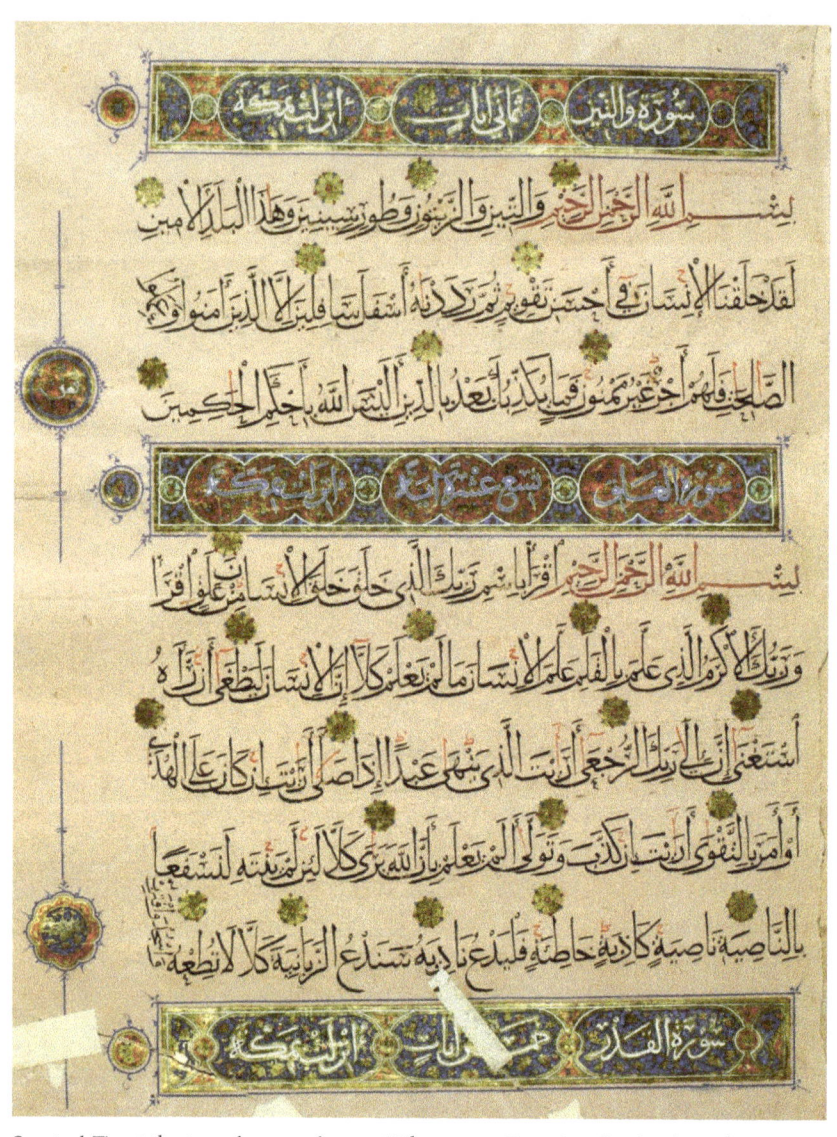

Suratu l-Tin at the top of a page from a 15th century Egyptian Qur'an from the Victoria and Albert Museum.

Postscript

The ideas addressed in the conclusion are expressed in Chapter 95 of The Qur'an, Suratu l-Tin, which condenses them amazingly into just a few words. The Arabic language is dense with meaning. Each word derives from a three-letter root which produces a family of permutations, that conjure up a host of verbal images and associations. This constellation of meanings was undoubtedly available to the people of the Prophet's (sas) time who placed a high value on poetry which is the ultimate art of linguistic distillation. From reading the tafsir of the experts, insha' Allah, we can partake of this knowledge and expand the horizons of our own understanding.

[The following interpretation is based on the Tafsirs of as-Suyuti, of Maybudi, and of Ibn Kathir. The definition and derivations of the words are from the Arabic-English Lexicon of Edward Lane.]

By the fig and the olive,
By the mount of Sinai
And this land of safety (*baladi l-amin*),
Truly We created man in the best of forms (*taqwim*).
Then We returned him to the lowest of the low (*safilin*)
Except for those who believe and do good deeds. For them is a reward unending.
So why do you still reject the *din*?
Is Allah not the most wise of those who judge (*hakim*)?

["*Balaa*" – "Yes indeed. I am of those who bear witness." This is what the Prophet (sas) told us to say after reciting the verse above.]

By the land of **the fig**, which is a tree of Paradise. The fig is associated with the ancient land called Syria, the land of the earliest revelations of the divine law, that of Nuh (as), whose Ark landed on Mount Judi, and of Adam (as), whose nakedness was covered by the fig tree's gift and who dwelled for a time on Mount Qasyun (Damascus).

And of **the olive** – Jerusalem, Canaan, which is the land of Ibrahim (as) and the prophets after him until 'Isa (as). The Mount of Olives outside of Jerusalem is holy to both Jews and Christians. Many prophets and saints are buried there and the Jews believe it is where the Day of Resurrection will begin. 'Isa (as) prayed and taught there and is believed to have ascended to heaven from there.

And by Mount Sinai – where the Law, the Tawrah, was given to mankind by means of Musa (as), Harun (as), and Yusha' (as).

And by this sanctuary (baladi l-amin) – Mecca, Medina which is the land of Muhammad (sas), who himself was called al-Amin (sas).

Taqwim – which is derived from the root q-w-m meaning upright, upstanding, ordered, balanced and steady; the orderly arrangement of the stars, a calendar, an equation; to be devoted to, or mindful of an affair, to appreciate the value of something and to take good care of it (**the man is qawwamuna over the woman** 4:34). Islam is **ad-dinu l-qayyim**, the upright religion 9:36, 12:40, 30:30, 30:43, 98:5. Al-Qa'im is a title of the Mahdi (as).

Safilin – derived from the root s-f-l meaning to be low, the undercarriage of an animal, ignoble, unjust, without value.

Din – derived from the root d-y-n meaning to obey, submit, be a slave, be in debt; the path of obedience.

Hakim – derived from the root h-k-m meaning to prevent from doing evil or behaving ignorantly; a wise person or judge.

Allah Almighty links the holy places together, from north to south. These are the places where He has chosen to connect the spiritual and physical worlds and to reveal His guidance to His chosen Messengers. He adjures by them that He has created mankind, like the heavens, in the most perfect, balanced state, to be His deputies, the caretakers of creation. But mankind persists in choosing the lowest, most ignoble state of being. Allah created the body of man from dust and He returns it back to dust but man himself chooses for his soul an even lower station by obeying his animal self rather than his loving Lord. That is, except for those who reach for the stars, who believe in Allah and His messengers and act righteously, for they will receive the reward of eternity. So, knowing this, why are you still opposed to the way of obedience laid out in the Books and exemplified by the Messengers? Isn't Allah certainly the most just and wise of any who have ever wanted to prevent you from acting ignorantly and from doing harm to your own selves?

Balaa! Yes! I bear witness.

Glossary

Abdal – A high order of saint, called the substitutes.

Abu Bakr (ra) – The father-in-law and close companion of the Prophet Muhammad (sas) and the first rightly guided khalif in Islam.

'Ali ibn Abi Talib (ra) – The fourth rightly guided khalif and the cousin of the Prophet (sas) and his son-in-law.

Alif – The first letter in the Arabic alphabet corresponding to 'A'. The first letter in the name Allah. The long vertical bead on a misbaha that joins both ends together.

Al-Yasa' (as) – The prophet Isaiah.

Arhamu r-Rahimin – Epithet for Allah, the Most Merciful of the merciful.

Ariha – Jericho, a major city today in the so-called West Bank of Israel; an ancient site of habitation dating back to the bronze age.

Asiya (rah) – The wife of Pharaoh and the adopted mother of Musa (as).

Ash-Sham – All the land within a radius of 6 days by camel from Damascus. Canaan, Palestine, Mesopotamia.

As-Samiri – The builder of the golden calf.

Awliya – The plural of *wali*, meaning protecting friends, saints.

Awtad – A classification of saint called the stakes or supports.

'Aysha (rah) – The wife of the Prophet (sas) and daughter of Abu Bakr (ra).

'Azra'il (as) – Pronounced Azra-eel. One of the four Archangels called in The Qur'an the Angel of Death, Maliku l-mawt.

Banu Isra'il – The Children of Isra'il (as) or Jacob, the tribes descending from the 12 sons of Jacob (as), the Jewish people.

Barzakh – The place where the souls reside after death and before Judgment Day, an in between place.

Beykoz – A town in Anatolia overlooking the Bosporus with a maqam for Yusha' (as).

Al-Bukhari – His collection of Hadith of the Prophet (sas) is one of the most authoritative. He died in 810 CE in Bukhara.

Buraq (as) – The heavenly steed which carried the Prophet Muhammad (sas) on the Night Journey.

Canaan – The land promised to the descendants of Ibrahim (as) by Allah Almighty, Palestine, most of what is called Israel today, the Holy Land, *Bilad ash-Sham*.

Cosbi – The daughter of the king of Balqa who committed adultery with Zimri.

Dawud (as) – The prophet David, pronounced Dawood.

Dhikr – Meaning to remember, also the ritual remembrance of Allah.

Dhu l-Kifl (as) – Meaning Possessor of the Fold or Division. One of the possible names for Yusha' (as).

Dhu l-Qarnain (as) – A prophet mentioned in The Qur'an, "the Possessor of the Two Horns", usually identified with Alexander the Great.

Du'a – Prayer in the sense of asking for something, making a plea.

Fata – *Fityatun* pl. Allah's champions, chivalrous youths, knights, spiritual warriors.

Fatima (rah) – The Prophet Muhammad's (sas) youngest daughter and the wife of Sayyiduna 'Ali (kw).

Fatwa – Judicial ruling.

Fin'has (ra) – Phineas, a grandson of Harun (as) who inherited the role of high priest. His name is another thought to be derived from ancient Egyptian rather than Hebrew: pa-nehasi, the southerner.

Fitra – The natural state in which Allah made us, submitted to Him.

Futuwwa – The path of spiritual struggle, nobility, chivalry.
Al-Ghazali - Scholar and Sufi. Died 1111 CE in Iran.
Habib Allah – The Beloved of Allah – an honorific of the Prophet Muhammad (sas).
Habil (as) – Pronounced Habeel – Abel, the son of Adam (as).
Hadith – The transmitted and recorded words and actions of the Prophet Muhammad (sas) that have been ranked and rated by the scholars according to their veracity.
Hajar (rah) – The second wife of Ibrahim (as) and the mother of Isam'il (as).
Hajj – The annual pilgrimage to Mecca.
Hanif – Pronounced haneef from the root h-n-f – to incline towards. One inclining to truth, a true believer.
Harun (as) – Pronounced Haroon, the prophet Aaron, the older brother of Musa (as).
Hasan al-Basri (q) – Sufi and scholar. Tabi'in born in Medina in 642 CE.
Hawwa (rah) – Eve, the first woman.
Hijab – Veil, or curtain, scarf.
Hijra – Emigration, journey, flight.
Holy of Holies – A term referring to the inner sanctum of the Temple which held the Ark of the Covenant.
Iblis – Pronounced Iblees, The name of shaytan, the devil.
Ibn Abbas (ra) – The cousin of the Prophet (sas) responsible for the transmission of many hadith.
Ibn Hanbal – Scholar and jurist; founder of the Hanbali Madhhab. Died 855 in Baghdad.
Ibn Ishaq – Born in Medina in 704 CE. Died in Baghdad 768 CE. Historian and writer of the earliest biography of the Prophet (sas).
Ibn Kathir – 1301 – 1373 CE Syria. Scholar and historian, student of Ibn Taymiyya.
Ibrahim (as) – Pronounced Ibraheem. The prophet Abraham (as).
Idris (as) – The prophet Enoch.
Ilyas (as) – The prophet Elijah.
Imam – One who stands in front, a leader, specifically the leader of prayer.

Imam Malik – 711 – 795 CE Medina. Muhaddith, scholar and jurist. Collected one of the earliest, most respected collections of hadith, the Muwatta.

Imam Muslim – Scholar and *muhaddith,* who composed one of the 6 major collections of verified hadith, Sahih Muslim. Died 876 CE Iran.

Iman – Meaning faith.

'Imran – The father of Musa (as). Pronounced Imraan.

Injil – Pronounce injeel, the Book of 'Isa (as), the Gospel.

'Isa (as) – Pronounced Eesa, the prophet Jesus.

Ishaq (as) – Pronounced Is-haq. The prophet Isaac.

Isma'il (as) – Pronounced Isma-eel. The prophet Ishmael.

Israa – A night journey, specifically the miraculous journey of the Prophet Muhammad (sas) from Mecca to Jerusalem.

Isra'il (as) – Pronounced Isra-eel. Israel, another name for the prophet Ya'qub, Jacob (as).

Israfil (as) – Pronounced Israfeel. The Archangel who will blow the trumpet at the end of time.

Jibra'il (as) – Pronounced Jibra-eel. The Archangel Gabriel who delivers God's words. Kaffir – one who denies the truth – an unbeliever.

Jihad – Struggle on the path of God, both inward and outward.

Judah (ra) – The oldest of the twelve sons of Ya'qub (as), of the Bani Isra'il.

Jumu'ah – Juma', Friday, the Sabbath of the Muslims.

Juz – Meaning 'part' in Arabic. The Qur'an is divided into thirty equal parts, one to be read each day of the month.

Ka'b al-Ahbar – 7th century Yemeni Jew who converted to Islam and served under the Khalifas 'Umar ibnu l-Khattab (ra) and 'Uthman ibn 'Affan (ra).

Al-Kahf – The Cave. The 19th Chapter of The Qur'an.

Khadija bint Khuwaylid (rah) – The Prophet Muhammad's (sas) first wife and the mother of his children.

Khalifa – Deputy, successor, ruler. Pronounced khaleefa.

Khalil – Pronounce khaleel. Meaning intimate friend from the root kh-l-l meaning to penetrate, permeate.

Khalilu r-Rahman – Pronounced khaleelu r-Rahmaan meaning friend of the All-Merciful, an title of the prophet Ibrahim (as).

Khandaq – The third battle of the Muslims of Medina against the Quraysh of Mecca, also called the Trench.

Khatm – The seal, the final one, the one who seals up, completes the category or the position.

Khaybar – An oasis in Arabia that was the site of a famous battle and victory of the Prophet (sas).

Khidr (as) – A saint and prophet mentioned in The Qur'an in relation to Musa (as). Also known as the Green Man said to have been given eternal life. Sometimes associated with Ilyas (as) Elias.

Kilab (ra) – Caleb. One of the two righteous spies and the husband of Musa's (as) sister Mariam (rah).

Lawi (ra) – Levi, the son of Jacob (as), founder of the tribe of Levites.

Madhhab – pl. *madhahib*. School of Law. There are now only four accepted Sunni schools – Hanifi, Shafi'I, Maliki, and Hanbali. There used to be hundreds of others but they have no more followers. The Shi'a also have their own school. They come to different conclusions on matters of Shari'ah all based on The Qur'an and Hadith.

Madyan – A country at the time of Musa (as) in the northern coast of Arabia.

Mahdi (as) – A member of the Prophet's (sas) family who will fight the antichrist at Armageddon, the messiah.

Mahshar – The place of gathering for judgment on Yawmu l-Qiyama.

Manna and *salwa* – some kind of grain and quails with which Allah Almighty provided the Banu Isra'il in the desert.

Maqam – Place, station, shrine, tomb.

Marwa – One of two small hills in Mecca, as-Safa and al-Marwa, between which pilgrims run, *sa'i*, in memory of Hajar (rah).

Maryam (rah) – The older sister of Musa (as).

Mashhad – A place where the spiritual essence of a holy person is present although it is not a gravesite.

Masih – Arabic for Messiah, Meshiach (Hebrew).

Masih ad-Dajjal – The Anti-Christ, the false messiah.

Midrash – Commentary on the Torah and stories of the Rabbis collected in the first ten centuries CE.

Mihrab – A niche indicating the direction of prayer in a mosque, or a small secluded place of prayer.

Mika'il (as) – Pronounce Mika-eel. The Archangel Michael who is responsible for the vegetation of the world and justice.

Mi'raj – The ascent to Heaven of the Prophet Muhammad (sas).

Misbaha – Prayer beads, rosary.

Mishna – Called the Oral Torah, it is like a tafsir of the Torah by Rabbis.

Muhammad Mustafa (sas) – Muhammad the Chosen one (sas).

Muharram – The first month of the Muslim (Hijri) year.

Musa (as) – Pronounced Moosa – The prophet Moses (as).

Mushrik – Meaning idolater, one practices shirk, to worship other than Allah.

Muslim – From the root *s-l-m* meaning peace, submission.

Al-Muwatta – The 8th century collection of hadith of Imam Malik.

Nabi – Meaning prophet. pl. anbiya.

Namrud – Nimrod, the tyrant who opposed the prophet Ibrahim (as) Abraham.

New Testament - Composed of 27 books that tell the story of 'Isa (as) and the first century Christians. The New Testament and the Old Testament combined are the holy scripture of the Christians, The Bible.

Nuh (as) – Pronounced Nooh, the prophet Noah.

Old Testament – It divided into 39 Books which are a different ordering of including the Torah and the books of Prophets and Wisdoms called the Tanakh by the Jews.

Palestine – Canaan, Ash-Sham. The land promised Ibrahim (as), Mesopotamia.

Pharaoh – King of Ancient Egypt.

Qabil – Pronounced Qabeel – Cain the son of Adam (as).

Qarun – Koreh in the Bible. A wealthy member of the Banu Isra'il who opposed Musa (as). Pronounced: Qaroon.

Qibla – The direction faced in prayer.

Qiyama – Arising, the Day of Resurrection.

Al-Qushayri – Born 986 and died 1074 CE Khorasan. Scholar and sufi.

Quraysh – The tribe to which the Prophet (sas) belonged, descendants of Isma'il (as).

Qutb – Meaning pole or pivot. The head of the hierarchy of saints.

Rabb - Meaning Lord, Sustainer, the One who nourishes.

Rahab (rah) – The Canaanite woman who saved the spies of the Banu Isra'il.

Rahma – Compassion.

Al-Rahm – The womb.

Rasul – Pronounced rasool, meaning messenger.

Ruku' – (pl. *raka'at*) The act of bowing in the Muslim prayer. Raka'in, those who bow in prayer.

Sadaqa – Charity

Safa - One of two small hills in Mecca, Safa and Marwa, between which pilgrims run, sa'i, in memory of Hajar (rah).

Saffura (rah) – The wife of Musa (as) and daughter of Shu'ayb (as). Called Zipporah or Tsipporah in Hebrew.

Sajda – The act of prostration in the Muslim prayer.

Sakhra – rock, particularly the rock under the Dome of the Rock in Jerusalem.

Salah - Prayer

Salam – Pronounced salaam. Meaning peace and also to be submitted to God.

Salman al-Farsi (ra) – One of the close companions of the Prophet Muhammad (sas) of Persian Zoroastrian origin who searching for the true religion was enslaved and brought to Medina where he met the Prophet (sas) and became Muslim.

Sayyid – Master, lord.

Sayyida – Mistress, lady.

*Sayyidun*a – Pronounced sayyidina, our master.

Sayyidatuna – Pronounced sayyidaatina, our lady.

Shari'ah – Islamic Law derived from The Qur'an and Hadith by exceptional men of great learning and understanding. A place where a confluence of rivers has made an open valley.

Shaytan – Satan, the devil.

Shem (as) – Son of Noah (as) ancestor of the Semites.

Shu'ayb (as) – The prophet Jethro, the father-in-law of Musa (as) sent to the people of Midian.

Siddiq – A man of truth.

Siddiqah – A woman of truth.

Sirah – Meaning life or journey, it refers to a history or biography.

Sirat – The razor thin bridge over Hell that must be crossed safely in order to reach Paradise.

Al-Suhrawardi – Shihab ud-Din, scholar and sufi. Born 1154 in Iran, died 1234 in Syria.

Sulayman ibn Dawud (as) – The prophet Solomon son of the prophet David.

Sunnah – The practices and example of the Prophet Muhammad (sas) as recorded in the Hadith.

As-Suyuti – Egyptian scholar, jurist, historian, 1445 – 1505 Cairo.

Surah – Chapter of The Qur'an.

Tabut – The Ark of the Covenant.

Tafsir – Explanation, interpretation, exegesis of The Qur'an.

Tahnik – The practice of the Prophet (sas) of feeding a newborn a small piece of date.

Talmud – Rabbinical commentaries on Jewish the law and tradition written after the Babylonian exile.

Tanakh – What the Christians call the Old Testament consisting of the Torah, History, Prophets, and Wisdoms.

Tawaf – Circumambulation around the Ka'ba.

Tawrah - Torah – The Law as revealed to Moses in the 5 books of Moses – Genesis, Exodus, Leviticus, Numbers, and Deuteronomy called by Christians the Pentateuch, part of the Old Testament.

Tirmidhi – Scholar and muhaddith, 824 – 892 CE Uzbekistan. He compiled one of the 6 canonical collections of Hadith.

Uhud – The second battle fought by the Muslims of Medina against the Quraysh of Mecca.

'Umar (ra) – Sayyiduna 'Umar ibnu l-Khattab (ra) a close companion of the Prophet (sas) and the second rightly guided khalif of Islam.

Ummah – Nation, community.

'Umra – The ritual visit to Mecca that can be accomplished at any time of the year.

Uways al-Qarani (ra) – A companion of the Prophet (sas) who never physically met him but with whom he had a spiritual connection.

'Uzayr (as) – Pronounced Oozayr, the prophet Ezra.

Wahb ibn Munabbih (ra) – A Yemeni convert to Islam, 655 – 738 CE. Some say of Jewish origin. He collected many of the stories of the prophets.

Wali – A protector, a saint, a friend of Allah.

Walid – Pronounced waleed – birth parent.

Wudu' – Ablution, ritual washing in preparation for prayer.

Yahweh – Jehova, Ya Hu, "I am He who is", the spoken form of YHWH.

YHWH – The unutterable name of God, the tetragrammaton.

Ya'juj and Ma'juj – Gog and Magog. Two tribes of ravenous creatures who will appear at the end of time and devour everything.

Ya'qub (as) – Pronounced Ya-coob, the prophet Jacob.

Yawmu l-Qiyama – The Day of Arising, the Resurrection.

Yuchabad (rah) – The mother of Moses (as).

Yunus (as) – The prophet Jonah.

Yusha' (as) – The prophet Joshua.

Yusuf (as) – The prophet Joseph.

Zakah – Tithe, tax, giving a prescribed amount of your wealth once a year to be used for those in need. Derived from the root meaning 'to grow'.

Zimri – The tribal leader of the Banu Isra'il who was punished for adultery.

Zuhd – Asceticism, renunciation of the world. Sayyiduna Ali (ra) said "a zahid is not one who owns nothing but rather one who is owned by nothing."

Bibliography

Translations of The Qur'an

I have used all the following translations interchangeably throughout the text, sometimes one, sometimes another depending on which seems most appropriate or most graceful. Where it occurs, I have taken the liberty to change archaic vocabulary, such as thou to you etc.

Abdel Haleem, M.A.S. trans. *The Qur'an*. Oxford: Oxford University Press, 2004.
Ali, A. Yusuf. trans. *The Holy Qur'an*. NY: Aftner Publication, 1946.
Asad, Muhammad trans. *The Message of the Qur'an*. Gibraltar: Dar al-Andalus, 1980.
Nasr, Seyyed Hussein editor. *The Study Quran*. New York: Harper Collins, 2015.
Pickthall, Marmaduke trans. *The Meaning of the Glorious Qur'an*. London: Allen & Unwin Ltd., 1930.
Islamicity Qur'an Search provides 10 different English translations of each ayah. https://www.islamicity.org/quransearch/

General Bibliography

Abbas, Hasan. *The Prophet's Heir: The Life of Ali ibn Abi Talib*. New Haven: Yale University Press, 2021.

Addas, Claude. "The Muhammadian House: Ibn 'Arabi's Concept of *ahl al-bayt*." in Journal of the Muhyiddin Ibn 'Arabi Society, vol. 50 2011, 77-95.

Adil, Hajjah Amina. *Lore of Light*. MI: Institute for Spiritual and Cultural Advancement, 2009

Adil, Hajjah Amina. *Muhammad – Messenger of Islam*. Washington D.C.: ISCA, 2002

Akkach, Samir. "The Poetics of Concealment: Al-Nablusi's Encounter with the Dome of the Rock." Accessed from: https://www.academia.edu/9542531/THE_POETICS_OF_CONCEALMENT_AL_NABULUSI_S_ENCOUNTER_WITH_THE_DOME_OF_THE_ROCK

Arraf, Jane. "Tomb of Joshua, Revered Prophet, Beckons Believers in Baghdad." 20/2/2021. Accessed from: https://www.nytimes.com/2021/02/20/world/middleeast/baghdad-iraq-joshua-tomb.html

Ayten, Ali and Ali Köse. "Muslim Holy Sites in Istanbul: Shrines." Accessed from: https://istanbultarihi.ist/545-muslims-holy-sites-in-istanbul-shrines

Bible Walks. "Tibneh – Ancient Timna." Accessed from: https://www.biblewalks.com/tibneh#JoshuaTomb

Beegle, Dewey M. "Moses, Hebrew Prophet." Britannica. Accessed from: https://www.britannica.com/biography/Moses-Hebrew-prophet

Chittick, William C. "Ibn 'Arabi's Own Summary of the *Fusus*: "The Imprint of the Bezels of Wisdom"" Journal of the Muhyiddin Ibn 'Arabi Society, vol. 1 1982. Accessible from: https://ibnarabisociety.org/wp-content/uploads/PDFs/Chittick_Fusus-summary.pdf

Cohen, Shaye. "The Origins of the Matrilineal Principle in Rabbinic Law," AJS Review 10, 1 (Spring 1985). Accessed from: http://www.jstor.org/stable/1486271

Corbin, Henry. *The Man of Light in Iranian Sufism*. Boulder: Shambala, 1978.

Corbin, Henry. *Temple and Contemplation*. England: Islamic Publications Ltd., 1986.

Crawford, John S. "Caleb the Dog". Bible Review, April 2004 vol. 20, issue 2. Accessed from: https://www.baslibrary.org/bible-review/20/2/6

Creach, Jerome F. D. *Joshua*. Louisville: John Knox Press, 1989.

Davidson, Baruch S. "Why Is Joshua Referred to in the Torah as 'bin' Nun?" Accessed from: https://www.chabad.org/parshah/article_cdo/aid/533436/jewish/Why-Is-Joshua-Referred-to-As-Bin-Nun.htm

Doak, Brian R. *The Last of the Rephaim: Conquest and Cataclysm in the Heroic Ages of Ancient Israel*. Dissertation presented to the Department of Near Eastern Languages and Civilizations, Harvard University April 2011. Accessed from: https://digitalcommons.georgefox.edu/cgi/viewcontent.cgi?article=1002&context=ccs

El-Khatib, Abdullah. *Jerusalem in the Qur'an*. British Journal of Middle Eastern Studies Vol. 28, No. 1 (May, 2001), pp. 25-53. Accessed from: https://www.jstor.org/stable/826193?seq=1

Al-Ghazali, Abu Hamid Muhammad. *Mukhtasar ihya 'ulum as-din*. Marwan Khalaf trans. Nikosia: Spohr Publishers Ltd., 2013.

Ginzberg, Louis. *Legends of the Bible*. Philadelphia: The Jewish Publication Society of America, 1992.

Grabar, Oleg. "The Story of Portraits of the Prophet Muhammad." Studia Islamica 96, (2003): 19-38. https://www.academia.edu/23289201/The_Story_of_Portraits_of_the_Prophet_Muhammad

Grabar, Oleg. *The Shape of the Holy*. Princeton: Princeton University Press, 1996.

Guenon, Rene. *Lord of the World*. England: Coombe Springs Press, 1983.

Guenon, Rene. *Fundamental Symbols: The Universal Language of Sacred Science*. Compiled and Edited by Michel Valsan. Revised by Martin Lings. Cambridge: Quinta Essentia, 1995.

Guillaume, A. *The Life of Muhammad: a translation of Ibn Ishaq*. Oxford University Press. Pakistan, 1955

Haddad, Gabriel Fouad. *The Rightly-Guided Caliphs and the Four Imams*. Damascus, 1998.

Haddad, Gabriel Fouad. "Sayyidina 'Ali ibn Abi Talib (r)." Accessed from: https://sunnah.org/2016/09/28/sayyidina-ali-ibn-abi-talib-r/

Halman, Hugh Talat. *Where the Two Seas Meet: Al-Khidr and Moses The Qur'anic Story of al-Khidr and Moses in Sufi Commentaries as a Model for Spiritual Guidance.* USA: Fons Vitae, 2013.

Hazluck, F.W. and Margaret M. Hazluck. *Christianity and Islam Under the Sultans.* Vol. 1. Oxford: Clarendon Press, 1929. Accessed from: https://www.academia.edu/40487065/CHRISTIANITY_AND_ISLAM_UNDER_THE_SULTANS_1

"The Identification of Pharaoh at the Time of Moses." Accessed from: https://www.islamic-awareness.org/quran/contrad/external/mosespharaoh.html

Ibn Abbas, Abdullah. *Tanwir Al-Miqbas.* Accessed from: https://www.altafsir.com

Ibn 'Arabi, Muhiyiddin. *The Bezels of Wisdom.* R. W. J. Austin trans. NY: Paulist Press, 1980.

Ibn 'Arabi, Muhiyiddin. *The Meccan Revelations.* M. Chodkiewicz ed. NY: Pir Press, 2005.

Ibn Ishaq. *The Life of Muhammad.* A. Guillaume trans. Lahore: Oxford University Press, 1974.

Ibn Kathir, Ismail. *Stories of The Prophets.* Riyadh: Maktaba Dar-us-Salam, 2003.

Ibn Kathir, Ismail. *Qur'an Tafsir* accessed from: http://www.qtafsir.com

Al-Kashani, Abd ar-Razaq. *Tafsir.* Accessed from: https://www.altafsir.com

Khan, Majid Ali. *The Pious Caliphs.* Kuwait: Islamic Book Publishers, 1978

Kisai, Muhammad ibn 'Abd Allah. *Tales of the Prophets.* Wheeler M. Thackston Jr. trans. USA: Great Books of the Islamic World, Inc., 1997.

Koenigsberg, Zvi. "Joshua's Altar on Mount Ebal: Israel's Holy Site Before Shiloh." Accessed from: https://www.thetorah.com/article/joshuas-altar-on-mount-ebal-israels-holy-site-before-shiloh

al-Lamati, Aḥmad ibn al-Mubarak. John O'Kane and Bernd Radtke trans. *Pure Gold from the Words of Sayyidi 'Abdal Aziz al-Dabbagh.* Leiden: Brill, 2007

Lane, Edward William. *An Arabic-English Lexicon.* London: Islamic Texts Society, 1984.

Lazaroff, Tova. "In Pictures: Thousands Hike at Midnight to Visit Joshua's Grave." The Jerusalem Post: 4/6/2016. Accessed from: https://www.jpost.com/israel-news/thousands-hike-at-midnight-to-visit-joshuas-grave-453057

Lings, Martin. *Muhammad His Life Based on the Earliest Sources*. Rochester VT: Inner Traditions International, 1983.

Lory, Pierre. "The Symbolism of Letters and Language in the Work of Ibn 'Arabī." Accessed from: https://ibnarabisociety.org/symbolism-of-letters-and-language-pierre-lory/

Mahmud, Muhammad Bin Kanvendshah Bin. *The Rauzat-Us-Safa*. E. Rehatske trans. London: Kessinger Publishing, 2010.

Malik, Imam. *Muwatta*. Accessed from https://www.searchtruth.com/searchHadith.php

Mark, Robert and Ahmet S. Çakmak eds. *Hagia Sophia from the Age of Justinian to the Present*. Cambridge: Cambridge University Press, 1992.

Miskinzoda, G. "The Significance of the Hadīth of the Position of Aaron for the Formulation of the Shīʿī Doctrine of Authority". Bulletin of the School of Oriental and African Studies, University of London vol. 78, no. 1. Accessed from: https://www.jstor.org/stable/24692177?seq=1

Muslim, ibn al-Hajjaj. *Sahih Muslim*. Accessed from: https://www.searchtruth.com/searchHadith.php

An-Nawawi, Imam Abu Zakariya Yahya. *Riyad As-Salihin*. Accessed from: https://sunnah.com/riyadussaliheen

Nebil, Husayn. "The Rehabilitation of ʿAlī in Sunnī Ḥadīth and Historiography." Journal of the Royal Asiatic Society, Series 3, 29, 4 (2019). Downloaded from: https://www.cambridge.org/core.

Norwood, J. W. "Fish and Water Symbols" The Open Court: vol. 1912; issue 11; article 3. Accessed from: https://opensiuc.lib.siu.edu/cgi/viewcontent.cgi?article=2705&context=ocj

Al-Rabghuzi, *The Stories of the Prophets*. Edited by H. E. Boeschoten and J. O'Kane. Leiden: Brill, 2015.

Renard, John. *Crossing Confessional Boundaries: Exemplary Lives in Jewish,*

Christian, and Islamic Traditions. Berkeley: University of California Press, 2020.

Renard, John. *Friends of God: Islamic Images of Piety, Commitment and Servanthood*. Berkeley: University of California Press, 2008.

Rippin, Andrew ed. *The Blackwell Companion to the Qur'an*. USA: Blackwell Publishing, 2006.

Rubin, Uri. "Muhammad's Night Journey (isra') to al-Masjid al-Aqsa: Aspects of the Earliest Origins of the Islamic Sanctity of Jerusalem." Accessed from: https://www.academia.edu/5617249/_Muhammad_s_Night_Journey_isra_to_al_Masjid_al_Aqsa_Aspects_of_the_Earliest_Origins_of_the_Islamic_Sanctity_of_Jerusalem_

Rubin, Uri. "Between Arabia and the Holy Land: A Mecca-Jerusalem Axis of Sanctity". Accessed from: https://www.academia.edu/6138286/_Between_Arabia_and_the_Holy_Land_A_Mecca_Jerusalem_Axis_of_Sanctity_

Rumi, Jalal ud-din. *The Mathnawi*. Translated and edited: Reynold Alleyne Nicholson. Tehran: Booteh Publications, 2002.

Al-Qushairi, Abd al-Karim. *Tafsir*. Accessed from: https://www.altafsir.com.

Schimmel, Annemarie. *The Mystery of Numbers*. New York: Oxford University Press, 1993.

Shah-Kazemi, Reza. *Imam 'Ali: from Concise History to Timeless Mystery*. London: The Matheson Trust, 2019.

Shelton, Mahmoud. *The Red and the White*. USA: Temple of Justice Books, 2019.

Shelton, Mahmoud. *Sacred Geometry and the Paths of the Sun*. USA: Temple of Justice Books, 2021.

Sherif, Mohamed A. *Ghazali's Theory of Virtue*. Albany: State University of New York Press, 1975.

Sindawi, Khalid. "Link Between Joshua Bin Nun and 'Ali Ibn Abi Talib." Ancient Near East Studies, vol. 47, 2010.

Smith, Johnathan Z. *To Take Place: Toward Theory in Ritual*. Chicago: The University of Chicago Press, 1987.

Sperling, Karima. *The Story of Moses*. USA: Little Bird Books, 2013.

Stelzer, Steffan. *The Freedom to Serve: Lectures of Shaikh Nazim.* Nikosia: Spohr Publishers Ltd, 2019.

As-Suyuti, Jalaluddin. *Tafsir al-Jalalayn.* Accessed from: https://www.altafsir.com

Al-Tabari, Abu Jafar Muhammad b. Jarir. *The History of al-Tabari vol. IV.* Moshe Perlmann trans. Albany: SUNY, 1987.

Tamtam, Hamza Elhadi Mohamad. *The Impact of the Figure of Khidr on Medieval Sufi Thought.* Thesis submitted to the Department of Theology and Religion, University of Birmingham, May 2019. Accessed from: https://etheses.bham.ac.uk/id/eprint/9336/7/Tamtam2019PhD.pdf

Al-Tha'labi, Abu Ishaq Ahmad b. Muhammad Ibrahim. *'Ara'is al-Majalis Qisas al Anbiya or Lives of the Prophets.* W. M. Brinner trans. Leiden: E. J. Brill, 2002.

Tihrani, Allamah Hajj Sayyid Muhammad Husayn Husayni. *Knowing the Imams. Vol. 4.* Chicago: Kazi, 2016.

Al-Tustari, Sahl. *Tafsir al-Tustari.* Accessed from: https://www.altafsir.com.

Twinch, Cecilia. "Created for Compassion". Accessed from: https://ibnarabisociety.org/dhu-l-nun-created-for-compassion-cecilia-twinch/

Vamosh, Mariam Feinberg. Sign of the Sea Squill. Accessed from: https://miriamfeinbergvamosh.com/sign-of-the-sea-squill/

van Kooten, George H. and Jacques van Ruiten eds. *The Prestige of the Pagan Prophet Balaam in Judaism, Early Christianity and Islam.* Leiden: Brill, 2008.

Wadeed ud-Din, Fakir Syed. *The Benefactor and the Rightly-Guided.* Chicago: Kazi Publications, 1995.

Al-Wahidi. *Asbab al-Nuzul.* Accessed from: https://www.altafsir.com

Wallace, Jennifer. "Shifting Ground in the Holy Land" Smithsonian Magazine May 2002. Accessed from: https://www.smithsonianmag.com/history/shifting-ground-in-the-holy-land-114897288/

Wensinck, Arent Jan. *The Ideas of the Western Semites Concerning the Navel of the Earth.* Amsterdam: J. Müller, 1916. Accessed from: https://dwc.knaw.nl/DL/publications/PU00010173.pdf

Wheeler, Brannon M. *Prophets in The Qur'an: An Introduction to the Qur'an and Muslim Exegesis*. London: Continuum, 2002.

Wheeler, Brannon M. *Arab Prophets of the Qur'an and Bible*. Journal of Qur'anic Studies, vol. 8, no. 2 (2002). Edinburgh University Press. Accessed from http://www.jstor.org

Wiesel, Elie. "Joshua in the Bible." Accessed from: https://www.biblicalarchaeology.org/daily/biblical-topics/hebrew-bible/joshua-in-the-bible/

Wilford, John Noble. "Believers Score in Battle Over the Battle of Jericho." 22/02/90 Accessed from: https://www.nytimes.com/1990/02/22/world/believers-score-in-battle-over-the-battle-of-jericho.html

Williams, Cheri. The "Hornet" of the Conquest in Deuteronomy 7:20: An Alternate Meaning. Accessed from: https://www.ancient-hebrew.org/biblical-history/the-hornet-of-the-conquest.htm

Winter, Tim. "The Chador of God on Earth: the Metaphysics of the Muslim Veil." New Blackfriars vol. 85, no. 996 (March 2004). Accessed from: https://www.jstor.org/stable/43250804?seq=1

Wood, Bryant G. The Walls of Jericho. Accessed from: https://biblearchaeology.org/research/conquest-of-canaan/3625-the-walls-of-jericho

Picture Credits

p.7 iStock mycan https://www.istockphoto.com/photo/a-turkish-horse-gm641195438-116376351
p.8-9 https://www.knowingthebible.net/bible-maps
p.10 Abu Simbel temple in Egypt. Shutterstock, Csilla Peter
p.32 Original artwork by Yoram Ranaan taken from https://religionnews.com/2020/08/28/ashura-muslims-recall-moses-pharaoh-christchurch-mosquer/
p.35 iStock kertu__ee https://www.istockphoto.com/photo/proud-camel-mother-walking-with-her-baby-gm925353906-253938661
p.40 Shutterstock Kochneva Tetyana https://www.shutterstock.com/image-photo/sunset-over-sacred-mount-moses-sinai-1233304312
p.47 Shutterstock Mountains Hunter. https://www.shutterstock.com/image-photo/beautiful-starry-sky-over-mountains-sinai-1326524861
p.54 http://www.fatherjustinsblog.info/archives/3429
p.136 https://madainproject.com/mount_ebal_altar#gallery-4
p.139 https://www.mq.edu.au/__data/assets/pdf_file/0020/178220/Map-04-Comprehensive-database-of-maps-from-BibleOnline.pdf
p.181 Painting by Alia Nazeer

www.ingramcontent.com/pod-product-compliance
Lightning Source LLC
Chambersburg PA
CBHW040317170426
43197CB00021B/2947